THE TREE FORAGER

Adele Nozedar

Illustrations by Lizzie Harper

WATKINS
Sharing Wisdom Since 1893

This book is dedicated to

Amanda Rudman,
"to whom I owe the leaping delight
that quickens my senses".
With love, Dominic

The Tree Forager
Adele Nozedar

First published in the UK and USA in 2021 by
Watkins, an imprint of Watkins Media Limited
Unit 11, Shepperton House,
83–93 Shepperton Road
London N1 3DF

enquiries@watkinspublishing.com

COMMISSIONING EDITOR: Fiona Robertson
EDITOR: Ingrid Court-Jones
EDITORIAL ASSISTANT: Brittany Willis
HEAD OF DESIGN: Glen Wilkins
COMMISSIONED ARTWORK: Lizzie Harper
PRODUCTION: Uzma Taj

A CIP record for this book is available
from the British Library

ISBN: 978-1-786785-47-3 (Hardback)
ISBN: 978-1-786785-74-9 (eBook)

10 9 8 7 6 5 4 3 2 1

Printed in China

www.watkinspublishing.com

CONTENTS

Foreword: The Sound of a Tree 6
Introduction: Connecting with Trees 8

FOREWORD:
The Sound of a Tree

You might think the idea of there being a connection between trees and music is quite obscure, even esoteric. But if you're lucky enough to grow up, as I did, surrounded by forests and able to create music, you'll know that it makes a lot of sense. In fact, even without these advantages, it's true. Let me tell you why.

Outside my home there's a large parking place, and right in the middle there's a big old chestnut tree. Recently, on a bright morning, I saw a stranger with her arms wrapped around the tree, hugging it passionately; the hug lasted for such a long time that I actually felt quite awkward watching the ritual. But it made me think that perhaps I'd do the same if I didn't have music to express my connection to the trees and the forests.

The smell, the light, the sound and the pure existence of trees has been a part of my being for a long time – since forever. I remember taking long, long walks with my father and my family into the woods. The amount of time that I have on earth, set against the perspective of the age of the forest, always gives me a feeling of great humbleness, making me feel grounded, connected to the moment, inhaling the essence of the might and beauty of the trees, inhaling every portion of oxygen that they give us.

I get that same "utterly alive" feeling when I sit on my bench in front of a grand piano. I use a technique called "prepared piano", in which lots of unexpected items are placed inside the body of the instrument – from sweet wrappers to ping-pong balls to things you've picked up from the ground. The audience watches me experiment with sounds, creating the sound of cracking wood, the rattling of leaves or the knocking of a woodpecker. Together, these sounds create a rhythmical texture that can be either in synch or else randomly arranged, complete chaos, an expression of one moment in that particular place. Even I don't always know exactly what's going to happen!

Music, for me, has always been about much more than melodies and harmonies. It is, in a way, nothing more or less than the combination of sounds in a certain place, either with, or without, an instrumentalist. So, the stage, without the pianist and before the concert, is already music. The piano tuner tuning the piano is also music. If I think about a walk in a forest, this is also music – with or without me. The rhythm of the bird song, the leaves, the breeze in the trees and all the other elements that create sound are very specifically connected with the place, creating a unique identity for that one particular moment.

Trees and music are, for me, rudimental elements in my existence, and the invitation to write this foreword has really made me think.

Thanks, Adele, for inviting me to share some thoughts.

Volker Bertelmann (Hauschka), 2021

Volker Bertelmann is a German pianist and composer who mainly performs and records under the name Hauschka. He is best known for his compositions for prepared piano.

INTRODUCTION:
Connecting with Trees

"The question is not what you look at, but what you see."
Henry David Thoreau (1817–62)

Like you (after all, you're reading this book), I have a deep, deep love of trees. They're gentle, magnanimous, always there, giving us so much even though we don't give them very much in return. They're so common that we often don't really notice them, and yet they're absolutely vital to life on this planet. This is why, as a forager, I realized I needed to turn my attention toward them, to gather them together as it were, in a celebration of their extraordinary ordinariness and their mind-blowing possibilities. And, of course, the sheer, breathtaking beauty of them.

I didn't randomly choose the trees I've included in this book; rather, they're trees I know personally, and which are part of my own story for various reasons. This is not a "normal" book about identifying trees and, dare I say, it's not a "normal" book about foraging, either. My aim in writing this book is simply to get you to notice trees. The more you take notice of trees, the more you'll find that you can't stop looking.

Trees may well become an obsession for you, as they have for me. As human beings, we are all tree foragers whether we realize it or not, and you'll recognize other members of our club by the interesting debris that we have in our pockets. X-ray vision would reveal something like the following:

- Unknown seeds, stuck grittily into the seams of the pocket
- A pinecone or two
- A small magnifying glass, in need of a polish
- A piece of stick with oakmoss attached

- A few acorns
- An oak apple
- A pencil stub
- A redundant key
- Dog biscuits

Does this sound similar? It's actually a bona fide inventory of my own pockets right now!

The Scent of a Tree

The book you are holding is about trees; even though the paper may be "wood-free", it is still made from trees. Could you do something for me? Bury your nose in this book and have a good, deep, noisy sniff. Isn't the scent delicious? When I worked in a bookshop, I knew that I would always like the customers who instinctively stuck their noses into a book, as you just did, not because they wanted to read it, but because they wanted to inhale that wonderful, fresh, new-book scent.

One day in the future, in about 60 years' time, this book – the one you are holding now – will smell different. It will smell even better; it will smell like an *old* book. That mellow, unmistakable scent, which I have tried (and failed) to replicate with various ingredients, is the aroma of pages gently rotting. If you pick up an old leaf from the leaf litter on a forest floor or one that's been buried in a compost bin for a while, you'll get a scent that's almost the same as that of an old book. And you'll suddenly realize why the pages of a book are also called leaves.

Listening to a Tree

There's another aspect of trees that I've noticed and never really spoken about until now, largely because I find it hard to explain. Somehow, trees and music are inextricably linked. I realize that this might seem quite an abstract concept, but as I've been writing this book, the idea has become more and more insistent. It was said that Gertrude Jekyll, the formidable and infamously eccentric writer, photographer, artist and garden designer, could recognize trees by the sound made by their leaves as the wind blew through them. Indeed, the sounds that trees make – the rattling of brittle leaves, the swooshing of boughs, the whispering susurration of a sudden breeze met by the rise and fall of a branch – have a music all of their own. They take what's given by the weather and conduct an orchestral score that's different every time, impossible to copy or repeat. And like the best kind of music, tree music carries you along with it, without you knowing what the orchestra will do next. I find, though, that it's in the elusive spaces, the silences among the sounds of a tree, that the true music lies.

You'll see that for each tree in the book I have chosen a song or a tune. You might think the songs are a good fit – or you might not. It doesn't matter. The idea is to try a different way of thinking. I have also put together a Spotify playlist, called "The Tree Forager", which is a collection of tree-related songs. It's open to collaboration, and I'd love to hear your choices!

Planting a Tree

I'm not going to go into detail about the damage our relentless human busyness is causing to the planet. Instead, with this book, I want to concentrate on what we *can* do on the most personal level, to bring back the balance and restore harmony. And since we are such an imaginative, problem-solving species, I've no doubt that we will find a way to do it.

The easiest place to start is by planting a tree. Not everyone has vast tracts of land in which to do this, but I can promise you that wherever you are there will be a tree conservation project near you. You could start, or join, a woodland group. My local one has been going for eight years now, meeting once a month. We manage the woodland sustainably, and the timber from fallen trees keeps the fires of twenty or so families going all year. As well as this, we get to spend a few carefree hours outside in the forest. It costs nothing. The Woodland Trust, based in the UK, supplies baby trees to community woodland groups like ours. And when you plant a tree, bear in mind that you are planting it for the entire world.

If you'd like to get involved with conservation, rewilding or tree planting projects, it makes sense to look at what is most local to you. In the USA, the American Forest Foundation, based in Washington DC, has spent three quarters of a century helping family forest owners to care for their land. And their work continues as, faced with growing threats to forests, it is more important than ever that family woodland owners actively steward their land.

In the UK, I'd like to highlight the work of the Penpont Project, a revolutionary restoration scheme that is led and managed by young people between the ages of 12 and 18. The project is not only about trees, but the bigger environmental picture, with a strong educational emphasis, too. Also close to me is another fabulous organization, Stump Up for Trees, which aims to plant a million trees in the area of the Brecon Beacons National Park, where I live. Which brings me to the dedication at the front of this book.

I wanted to be able to "pay back" some of the trees that were used in the physical manufacturing of this book. Normally the dedication would be written by me and illustrator Lizzie Harper, but we decided instead to raffle the opportunity for someone else to write it, with the proceeds going to Stump Up for Trees. Take a look on page 3 where the winner's chosen words are revealed!

How to Use This Book

There is no one, "correct" way to use this book. You might like to use it to help you identify trees, or read up about the wildlife they attract, their medicinal uses and folklore, and then make it your mission to find each species, one by one; or you may prefer simply to take a more ad hoc approach and just dip in and out as the fancy takes you. Above all I'd love this book to become a trusty companion you take with you on foraging trips that gets grubby with handprints and dog-eared from being in your pocket. I want you to enjoy it – and yourself – as well as the trees around you.

If you are new to foraging, a good place to start is by simply taking a walk through a place where there are trees. It doesn't need to be a heavily wooded area or an arboretum. Even in a city you can find amazing trees, often hidden in plain view. Their names don't matter. Just look at them, admire them and get to know them.

I hope, too, that you'll be inspired to try the recipes I've suggested – whether for food, herbal medicine or even ink – as well as the many diverse craft-making activities I've included.

Everything I do – whether it's a foraging walk, making gin blends from wild plants, encouraging kids to drag their parents out to find edible plants, or even writing books – is really only ever about one thing: getting people to see and appreciate what we have, right here, right now, on this planet that we are so incredibly lucky to be part of. This is a roundabout way of saying that this book is about much more than trees. It's about finding ourselves as we get to know a little bit more about our world. Although some of us might think otherwise, we're not special, we're not separate and we're definitely not superior to any other life form on this planet. We're inextricably linked to the natural world and its fate is our fate, too. That's my belief, anyway. I find this idea comforting – liberating, even.

I hope this book encourages you to spend time exploring and appreciating nature. But most of all, I wish that one day you will look at a tree you've seen a thousand times before and suddenly be blown away by it. You'll know when this happens – the magic will stay with you for the rest of your life.

Happy foraging!

Adele

Apple

Malus sylvestris and *Malus domestica* (ABOVE)

Song: "Hike" by Hauschka

When I was a kid, I was fascinated by the miniature apples that fell from the trees along the grass verge outside our house. In fact, I have just realized that these little apples were the very first wild food I ever foraged. I thought they were utterly magical, something from Alice's Wonderland and Narnia all rolled into one. The disappointment, though, came when I tried to eat one. Crab apples are generally mouth-puckeringly bitter, though not always. But because these were "my" apples, I pretended they were delicious anyway. Some crab apples are very palatable, especially if you're prepared for the worst.

The magical nature of the apple is recorded in folk tales and fairy tales (for example, Snow White was persuaded to take a bite of the beautiful, bright red, poisoned apple, and the Hesperides, the three nymphs in Greek mythology, guarded the golden apples). Also, you can cut an apple across the middle to reveal even more magic – a neat arrangement of five little pips that outline the shape of a five-pointed star, which as everyone knows, is the symbol of witches and sorcerers and which extrapolates most elegantly in nature as the Golden Spiral or the Golden Mean.

The names of old apple varieties read rather like a poem, especially if you say them out loud:

Worcester Pearmain, Beauty of Bath, King of the Pippins, Bloody Ploughman, Cornish Gilliflower, Egremont Russet, Keswick Codlin, Peasegood Nonsuch and Laxtons Superb, to name but a few.

What does it look like?

Malus sylvestris, also known as the crab apple or the forest apple, has a bushy appearance and can be found at the edges of forests or woodland. It grows to a height of 10m (33ft) with a similar spread. The true crab apple has thorns, a reminder that it belongs to the Rosaceae family that includes hawthorn, rowan and, of course, roses. These original wild crab apples are something of a rarity. The greyish, purply brown of the bark starts to flake as the tree grows older. Leaves are alternately spaced and oval-shaped, with pretty five-petalled blossoms, white, with a pink blush. After the blossoms have fallen, the small, rounded fruits grow to take their place. Malus domestica – the cultivated apple tree – grows up to 12m (39ft) tall, with fruits that are considerably larger than those of the crab apple.

But where did the first apples come from, and how did they spread throughout almost all temperate parts of the globe?

Malus sylvestris

The first apple trees came from Kazakhstan, near the Caucasus Mountains, at a place close to where the Garden of Eden is purported to have been (if it existed). This is the place where Eve, egged on by the mischievous serpent, offered Adam the only fruit that had been forbidden to them – the Fruit of Knowledge (often referred to as an apple). Things went very rapidly downhill from then on, as the pair realized they were naked, covered their embarrassment with the handy leaves of the fig tree (see page 65) and were exiled from the garden. It's an intriguing story, whether we choose to believe it or not. The apple that caused all the bother may well have been an ancient variety, *Malus sieversii*, the first apple to be cultivated, which still grows there. The name of the old capital of Kazakhstan, Almaty, means "full of apples" (*alma* means "apple").

The difference between a cultivated apple and a wild one is simply a matter of size. A crab apple can be up to 5cm (2in) across, whereas a cultivated one is generally bigger. Apples hybridize freely, hence there are more than 6,000 named varieties, and the seed of an apple is often very different from its parents. A naturally hybridized apple, often seen in the wild, is called a "wilding". We have developed a system called "grafting", which involves combining the lower part of a rootstock of one tree to the budding branch or "scion" of another tree, to maximize the qualities we desire in the apple fruit.

Malus domestica
"Kentish Fillbasket"

Apples arrived in the USA in the 18th century, where one particular character had a huge influence on their spread. John Chapman, known as Johnny Appleseed, was born in Leominster, Massachusetts, in 1774. Often portrayed as a tall, lanky man flinging apple pips from a bag, in truth his approach was far more methodical. An American pioneer, Chapman set up nursery orchards, then found people to tend them in return for a share of the apples. Essentially, he set up a franchise. Chapman was a born naturalist with an empathy for wild animals; one contemporary account states that, for a time, his travelling companion was a wolf whose leg he had healed. He was also thrifty, preferring to find ways of using things that would otherwise have been discarded. John Chapman died in 1845, and the street in which he was born was named after him.

Wildlife

Apples of all kinds are valuable to wildlife. You might not want bruised windfalls, but thrushes and other birds, as well as mammals such as squirrels, mice and voles, love them. Birds often nest in apple trees – look out for abandoned nests in the winter months after the leaves have fallen.

Medicinal Uses

There's truth in the saying "An apple a day keeps the doctor away." Eating a fresh, raw apple is good exercise for your gums and teeth, and the malic and citric acids in the fruits clean your teeth, too. These same acids stimulate your digestive system and help keep you "regular".

DEHYDRATED APPLE SLICES

Dehydrated apple slices are delicious, chewy and satisfying, a perfect snack when you fancy something sweet, but with the bonus of no added sugar. If you have your own crop of apples, that's great, but making the slices works just as well with apples that might have slightly passed their sell-by date. If you have a dehydrator, you'll know that it's useful for all sorts of things, but it's not essential. As the apple slices dry, their colour darkens and they shrink slightly. However you wish to dry them, slice as many as you can and spread them in a single layer to save on fuel.

Slice the apple as thinly as you can across its middle, starting at the stalk end (which can be discarded, as can the blossom end).

If using an oven, set to the lowest heat and leave the oven door open slightly to let moisture escape. Check after the first couple of hours. If using a dehydrator, set to a high temperature and cook for approximately 6 hours. Store in clean glass jars.

EASY APPLE BIRD FEEDER

Trees and birds are inextricably linked and encouraging birds into the garden means that you'll see lots more than usual, especially if you consistently put out food for them.

This is possibly the simplest feeder ever. All you need is a 20cm (8in) length of sturdy garden wire and an apple. Push the wire through the top of the apple and out of the bottom, then loop it up and twist. Next, loop the rest of the wire around a low-hanging branch that's close enough to watch the birds, but not close enough to scare them. After the birds have feasted on the apple, re-use the wire as often as you like.

CRAB APPLE VERJUICE

Also made with unripe grapes, verjuice is handy in cooking – or in cocktails – when you want a sharp flavour. Lemon juice works fine too, but this is a good way of using crab apples. Johnny Appleseed would be proud of you.

Makes about 400ml (14fl oz)

You will need:
1kg (2lbs 2oz) ripe crab apples
1 tbsp gin or vodka, as a
   preservative

A 400ml (14oz) glass bottle
   with a top

1. Wash the apples, pop them into a pan and cover them with water. Remove the apples and bring the water to the boil.
2. Then, put the apples in the boiling water, bring to the boil and cook for 1 minute.
3. Remove the fruit from the hot water, place in a sieve and run them under a cold tap.
4. When cool, extract the juice with a juice extractor or mash them and pass through a jelly bag (a bag made from fine but strong material, which you can hang over a tripod suspended over a bowl and let the liquid drip through).
5. Add the spirit, then funnel into the clean glass bottle. Store in the fridge.

Crab apples (and other apples that have a sharp, lemony taste) contain pectin, the substance that makes jams and jellies set. Rather than use shop-bought pectin, simply use de-pipped and mashed crab apples or use a juice extractor. Store in bags in the freezer.

Ash

Fraxinus excelsior

(This is the common ash, not to be confused with the mountain ash, which is another name for rowan)

Song: "Fake Plastic Trees" by Radiohead

A long, long time ago, I was a musician in a band. We weren't very good, to be honest, but we had a brilliant time (admittedly much of it when I should have been at school, but that's another story). One of our songs was based around a Greek myth, in which a tree nymph has no choice but to transform into vegetation – in this case, an ash tree – to escape the bestial clutches of Zeus. (This theme, by the way, is repeated time and time again with various other trees and plants).

When it came time to produce an album cover, some bright spark had the idea that I, as the only girl in the band, might be shown transforming from a fairly plump young girl of 18 or so (and definitely not at all sylph-like), into an almost-naked tree spirit. In the studio, not a bit of me was actually naked except for my head, arms and legs, but the horrors of image-editing did the rest. I also had an interesting time trying to mimic the face and profile of a girl turning into a tree (not easy), using a photo of an ash tree to determine its silhouette. It was a highly embarrassing episode, but the upside is that even now I can spot an ash tree immediately.

And what a lovely tree it is, too. Elegantly poised, with bark the trendiest grey-brown imaginable, the ash was also one of the sacred trees of the Druids, who named it Nuin, part of a trilogy of magical trees, along with the oak and the "thorn" (probably hawthorn). In Norse mythology, the name of the ash is Yggdrasil, the tree that reaches far up into the heavens and down to the underworld, where the Norns (the rulers of destiny) live. These stories underpin the importance in which we hold trees, since they tell us something of who we are and our place in the world.

Many trees are ascribed with healing powers of some sort. As the ash ages it sometimes develops holes that are large enough to climb into. According to folklore, if you had a poorly child, then passing the child, naked, through this hole and out of the other side was believed to be effective for a number of ailments.

The ash that I see most days is an odd specimen, all arms and legs, a bit like a skinny girl who is growing out of her clothes. One of the tallest branches bends over to touch the ground in several places, bumping up and down on particularly windy days. Another long branch sticks out at right angles from the trunk of the tree. Bundles of leaves grow directly from the trunk, dotted here and there, low enough to touch. It's not exactly a perfect specimen, which is probably why I like it.

The ash has many practical uses. It's very strong and shock absorbent, which means it's perfect for making items such as tool handles and hockey sticks. The wood is used for furniture, cricket stumps, sleds and bowls. One of the most innovative uses I've seen is the beautiful wooden-framed bicycles made by the Twmpa Cycles company. Seasoned ash burns cleanly, one of the best woods for a fire, while chipped and dried ash is particularly good for smoking in a barbecue. And as food? The really young pale green leaves are edible and make a good addition to a salad; the older, dried leaves can be made into a refreshing tea, and you can make a pickle from very young ash keys.

Fraxinus excelsior

What does it look like?

Deciduous, this tree grows to 30m (98ft) or more with a spread of 20m (66ft). The bark is smooth and pale grey, and it develops deep fissures as the tree ages. Leaves are 10cm (4in) long, opposite, pinnate (arranged on both sides of the stem) and tipped, with one extra leaf at the end. Ash has distinctive black buds sometimes called "witches' fingers". Tiny, petal-free purple flowers are borne in thick clusters, appearing in early spring before the leaves. The fruits – called *samara* – look like the bunches of keys. The ash is part of the Oleaceae family and therefore is a cousin of the olive.

Wildlife

Birds such as owls, woodpeckers and nuthatches like to nest in the ash. Because ash leaves are loose and airy, light can reach the ground, which allows wildflowers and plants such as dog violet and wild garlic to grow beneath the trees. In turn, these plants attract butterflies, bees and other pollinating insects.

Medicinal Uses

Ash was once used in the treatment of malaria and is still used as an anti-inflammatory by some medical herbalists because of its astringent properties ("astringent" means causing the contraction of skin cells). And some people swear that rubbing ash wood on a wart will make it go away. (I have no evidence as to whether or not this works.) See opposite for another ash remedy for warts.

SAMARA CHILLI PICKLE

Makes 1 medium jar

You will need:

250g (9oz) ash keys, washed and stripped from the stems
4 bay leaves
8 peppercorns
1–2 chillies, split (seeds included, depending on how hot you want the pickle to be)
1 tsp ground mace or cinnamon
½ tsp ground ginger
1 tsp salt
2 tbsp demerara (turbinado) sugar
500ml (17fl oz/2 cups) cider vinegar
A 300ml (10½oz) glass jar, sterilized

1. Put the keys into a pan, cover with water, bring to the boil and boil for 5 minutes.
2. Strain, refresh the water and repeat.

3. Allow to cool until you can handle the keys, then pack them into the warm, sterilized jar, leaving space for the other ingredients.
4. Put all the other ingredients into a heatproof bowl, then set the bowl into the pan, adding water to the pan. Bring to the boil and simmer for 5 minutes. Turn off the heat and leave the ingredients in the bowl to cool.
5. Strain the liquid and use to top up the jar of ash keys, shaking the jar so that there are no air bubbles.
6. Stand the jar in a cool dark place for a couple of months to let the flavours develop.

ASH WART REMEDY

There are hundreds, if not thousands, of ways of getting rid of warts. It seems that different people react to different cures, and that many of those cures simply cannot be explained by science. If you have warts, it won't do you any harm to try the following.

Simply prick the wart with a clean, sterilized pin, then stick the pin into a nearby ash tree, while reciting the following rhyme:

Ashen tree, ashen tree,
Pray buy these warts from me.

Presumably the pin is a sort of payment to the tree. If you feel this isn't enough, perhaps you could hang a thank you letter on the tree after the wart has disappeared.

Bay Laurel

Laurus nobilis

**Song: "Hounds of Love"
by Kate Bush**

What an intriguing tree this is! We know it has its origins in the Mediterranean Basin area, which was covered with dense forests of laurel at a time when the atmosphere was much wetter than it is now. As the ground dried out, so the laurel retreated, leaving space for more drought-tolerant plants. I had believed that laurel didn't like wet conditions, but, evidently, I'm wrong; so far, fingers crossed, they are thriving in pots right outside my front door, which is definitely a long way from a hot climate.

Those forests may have disappeared some ten thousand years ago, but we still have the legends about the bay laurel. In ancient Greece, the plant was called Daphne, after a young girl who was a priestess of Gaia, the Earth Mother, and was therefore bound to remain a virgin as long as she was a priestess. If you've read about the ash (see page 19), the following story might sound familiar. Apollo, the son of Zeus, was just as tediously lascivious as his father. When his attention turned towards Daphne, she asked the Earth Goddess for help. There are different versions of what happened next. One is that Gaia whisked Daphne off to Crete where she would be safe, and in her place left a laurel tree. So, Apollo got off lightly.

Since then, laurels have ensconced themselves more or less happily just about everywhere on the planet, and we use bay leaves as an essential herb in cooking. However, if you're buying a packet of them in a supermarket, they tend to be desiccated and flavourless. The scent of a fresh leaf, in contrast, is heavenly; tear it, rub it between your fingers and inhale its scent to get the full aroma. It is used as a base for many dishes in Indian cuisine; in European cooking it forms part of a bouquet garni (a little parcel of herbs: traditionally parsley, thyme and bay), which can be removed in its entirety after cooking. You'll find it in Caribbean cuisine, too, and it is also used in pickling. Bay is an indispensable ingredient in a simple white sauce. And try popping a leaf into your cafetière and letting it infuse for a few minutes with the coffee. Lovely.

How about non-food use? Bay oil can be used as a massage (aromatherapy) oil where it's good for everyday aches and pains; I discovered its warming properties were very effective when I was unable to walk far after a random gardening accident last year. The scent is deliciously soothing, too. Although it has a reputation for restoring thinning hair through being massaged into the scalp, I can't find any conclusive evidence for this. Why not find

What does it look like?

An evergreen tree with a naturally conical shape, the bay laurel grows to a height of 20m (66ft) with a spread of 10m (33ft). It has a shrubby growth pattern, with lots of stems emerging from the centre of the tree. The smooth, dark, oval leaves grow up to 10cm (4in) long, tapering at either end, and they have wavy edges. Male and female flowers occur on different trees, and the female plant bears black berries up to 1cm (½in) long. There are mixed reports as to whether or not these berries are edible, so the best bet is to leave them for the birds.

a bald friend and give it a go? Another indeterminate use of bay was as a means of seeing into the future. The Oracle of Delphi burned it to induce a trance-like state in order to access this useful information. Pliny the Elder warned that bay should never be used in a profane way. Culpepper, too, has this to say of bay, *"Bay… resisteth witchcraft very potently, as also all the evils old Saturn can do to the body of man … neither witch nor devil, thunder nor lightning, will hurt a man in the place where a bay-tree is."*

Laurus nobilis

Presumably, this is why bay trees were set either side of a door. I'm glad I put mine in the right place, although this was more for decoration than any other reason.

Wildlife
The dense thickets of well-established laurel make it a magnet for nesting birds. Nectar from the flowers provides food for several insects, including solitary bees, honeybees, and short-tongued bees.

Medicinal Uses
On a holiday in Crete, I discovered that, before World War II, itinerant collectors of bay leaves used to go from village to village, collecting the harvest. After extracting the oil from the leaves, they would sell the oil back to the villagers, who used it medicinally in a number of ways still prevalent today. The active components of bay leaves include vitamin A, used to improve the eyesight, as well as minerals such as calcium, potassium and iron. The lauric acid in the leaves is an insect repellant. An infusion of the oil is used

internally against flatulence as well as lack of appetite, and externally for relief of muscular stiffness and spasms.

BAY LEAF WATER

Simply put 30 fresh, clean leaves into a stainless-steel pan, cover with 1 litre (35fl oz/4¼ cups) of water, bring to the boil and simmer until the liquid is reduced by half. Add a few drops to dishes and homemade bread in the same way that you might use drops of vanilla in a dessert or a cake. Keeps for up to a month in the fridge.

BAY LEAF OIL INFUSION

Fill a 1-litre (35fl oz) glass jar with fresh, clean bay leaves and cover with a good-quality, neutral-flavoured oil (sunflower is good). Shake to make sure there are no air bubbles, then infuse for a month or so before removing the leaves and putting the oil into a smaller bottle. Can be used as a salad oil or dipping oil or turned into a soothing ointment that's good for aches, pains and strains (see below).

BAY LEAF OINTMENT

Makes 2 small jars

You will need:
50ml (1¾fl oz) infused bay leaf oil (see above)

50g (1¾oz) beeswax or solid coconut oil
2 x 50ml (1¾oz) glass jars

1. Put the infused oil and beeswax into a bain marie.
2. Mix together over a low heat, stirring.
3. Pour into clean jars, allow to solidify and use as necessary.
4. Store in a cool place.

BAY LEAF AND ELDER JELLY
by Gavin and Prue Kellett

I love this jelly and it's especially marvellous that it contains ingredients from two of the trees in this book.

Makes approximately 8 medium jars

You will need:
1kg (2lb 4oz) elderberries, stripped from the stems
16 fresh bay leaves
1kg (2lb 4oz) jam sugar
Juice of 1 lemon
5g (⅛oz) powdered pectin, to make the jelly set
8 x 200g (7oz) glass jars, sterilized

1. Put the berries and bay leaves into a heavy-bottomed pan with 1.5 litres (52fl oz/6½ cups) water.
2. Bring to the boil and simmer for 30 minutes, then leave overnight.
3. Strain and then measure the liquid. You'll need 1 litre (35fl oz/ 4¼ cups) in total so, if you're a little short, top up with water.
4. Combine the liquid, sugar, lemon juice and pectin in the pan and heat gently until the sugar is dissolved. Increase to a rolling boil for 15 minutes or until setting point is reached.
5. Test to see if the jelly is set by putting a blob on a cold saucer and leave for a minute. If the jelly wrinkles when pushed, then it's ready to pour into the warm, sterilized jars.
6. Seal when cold.
7. Spread thickly on toast or muffins, or dollop into porridge or yoghurt.

Beech

Fagus sylvatica

**Song: "Why May I Not Go Out and Climb the Trees?"
by Daniel Norgren**

Beech mast is edible and full of protein and minerals. Although better known as pig food, it has also been eaten by humans in times when other food is scarce. The botanical name of this tree – *fagus* – comes from a Greek word meaning "to eat" and, according to the ancient Greeks, mast was the first tree-based food eaten by humans. These little nuts aren't so popular these days, probably because of the time they take to gather and cook. It's not so very long ago, though, that beech mast was commonly used. Laura Ingalls Wilder, author of the

Little House on the Prairie books written in the 1930s, frequently used real incidents in her stories, describing in detail the tough lives of the pioneers. In one story she describes how, as a little boy, her husband Almanzo spent a whole day helping his father gather beechnuts to store for winter, he and his sister gorging themselves on them. The nuts were processed by the same thresher that the family used for all their oats, beans and grains.

Very fresh young beech leaves, too, are edible and silkily tender. If you can catch them at this stage, they are a good addition to salads.

One of the definitive features of the beech tree is its very smooth, grey bark. And if you see a tree with names carved into it, this is almost certainly a beech. Its bark is quite thin, so the carving

What does it look like?

An elegant tree up to 30m (98ft) tall, with smooth grey bark and oval leaves ... a description that fits quite a few trees. However, look a little closer. Do the leaves have a slightly wavy edge? Are they alternately spaced? If it's spring, are the leaves a clean, bright green, with slightly hairy edges? If it's autumn going in to winter, the leaves still on the branches may be a mix of buttery yellow and ginger turning to brown, with a crispy texture.

Tree identification, though, is not only about sight.

Be aware of the sound of your feet on the ground. Is there something crunchy underfoot? Look down into the leaf litter. If you see lots of little furry brown husks, like small wooden flowers with four petals enclosing three triangular nuts, then it's likely that you're standing underneath a beech tree. Beech mast (the collective term for tree fruits and nuts) is abundant and can be found scattered underneath the tree all year round.

"stretches" as the tree grows, deepening with the years. There's a huge old beech tree in the field where I walk my dog, with several names and dates carved into the bark. One of these carvings, a heart with an arrow through and the initials AW and WW, was done in the 1940s by the grandfather of someone I know, when courting the girl who became his wife.

Fagus sylvatica

The connection between beech and the written word doesn't end with bark carvings. Before paper began to be made in Germany in the 1300s, smooth beechwood slabs were used in the same way. *Buch*, the modern German word for book, is very similar to *Buche*, the word for beech. Because of this link to the written word, the tree is also associated with knowledge. As paper is often made from trees, the association is apt.

Beech trees live for at least 400 years, which means they become a much-loved part of the landscape for locals. Not so long ago there was a beech in a village not far from my home, outside an inn. This tree was at least 250 years old, huge, beautiful, and generously shaded the area on hot days. On winter nights the tree was lit up in different colours, a beautiful sight. Then the inn was sold. Within days of arriving the new owners hacked down the tree. The shock waves rippled through the community; people were really upset. What made things even worse was that the tree wasn't even used for anything, just shredded. There were a couple of successive tenant owners, neither of whom lasted long and the whole place is now abandoned. This is an example of how a tree can be an important part of a community, taken for granted until it's gone. What's interesting is that some people believe that the removal of the tree was somehow tied up with the failure of the business.

And in the sense that 250 years of goodwill was wiped out in a single day, they could be right. Anything else is just superstition. Isn't it?

Wildlife
The shady canopy of beech means that rare, shade-loving plants, such as the red helleborine, can grow beneath it. Caterpillars and moths, including the olive crescent, feast on the leaves. The tree's longevity means that it can get gnarly and knotty, which makes it attractive to wood-boring insects and birds.

Medicinal Uses
Beechwood tar – a by-product of the carbonization of other hardwoods such as oak, as well as beech – has a long history. It was used as glue from the middle Paleolithic to the early Mesolithic era, and there's evidence that it was used as a sort of chewing gum, too! More recently, it became an expectorant for chronic bronchial ailments in Europe, the UK and the USA. Further uses include as an ingredient in soaps and in the care of animals' hoofs and claws.

BEECH LEAF CRISPS
Serves 2

You will need:
A handful of fresh beech leaves
Cooking oil

Sea salt and freshly ground black pepper

1. Wash and dry the beech leaves thoroughly.
2. Pour enough oil into a pan to cover the leaves and get it hot.
3. Drop in the leaves, turning them quickly and carefully until they go crisp.
4. Lay them on kitchen paper and sprinkle with salt and pepper.
5. Serve straight away.

BEECH LEAF NOYEUX

A *noyeux* or *noyau* is a French term for a liqueur made from nuts, although this one is made from the fresh young green leaves of the tree. Be aware that the leaves are exactly right for only a short time.
Makes about 1 litre (35fl oz)

You will need:

3 large handfuls fresh young
  beech leaves
A 70cl (24fl oz) bottle of
  plain gin
225g (8oz/1 cup plus 2 tbsp)
  golden granulated sugar

200ml (7fl oz/¾ cup plus 2 tbsp)
  brandy
A 1-litre (35fl oz) glass jar with
  a plastic or glass lid

1. Remove any debris from the leaves and pop into the jar.
2. Cover with the gin, making sure that all the leaves are submerged (otherwise they will become discolored). If necessary, use an upturned saucer to keep them down.
3. Leave in the dark for a couple of weeks, then strain out the leaves.
4. Pop the sugar into a non-reactive pan with 300ml (10½fl oz/1¼ cups) water and bring to the boil.
5. Remove from the heat and let cool, then add to the gin.
6. Add the brandy, put the lid on the jar and leave for another couple of weeks for the flavours to develop.

A little goes a long way with this liqueur. We usually add a decent dash to the Christmas cake, but it's also good in the summer with soda water as a spritzer.

For a non-alcoholic version, simmer the leaves in water for 10 minutes, leave to cool completely and refrigerate for up to a week. Add ginger cordial, a squeeze of fresh lime, and a chunk of ice to taste.

Birch

Betula pendula (RIGHT)
and *Betula utilis*

**Song: "Two Silver Trees"
by Calexico**

The birch is a pioneer tree. This
means that it is among the first
trees to populate barren ground,
perhaps as a result of deforestation
or fire. A birch tree will pave the
way for other trees, shrubs and
plants, therefore making the
ground fertile. Birch grows all
over the planet, too, from densely
populated cities to vast tracts of
uninhabited land. There are many
different species of this tree,
including the downy birch (which is sometimes confused with the
silver birch). As you'd imagine from its name, the downy birch has
smooth, downy shoots. The colour of its bark is a dull brownish hue.
The botanical name of the Himalayan birch, *Betula utilis*, tells you
that this particular tree has a wide range of characteristics that have
made it useful to human beings, including being made into paper,
shoes, all manner of bowls, baskets and other containers, broom
handles and bobbins, as well as canoes and even skateboards. Let's
take a closer look at *Betula utilis* (which, in Sanskrit, is called *bhurja*,
which means "tree whose bark is used for writing upon" and is likely
to be the original name for the entire species). The bark of this tree
is particularly easy to peel away in long strips, and so was used as
paper from the 4th to the 16th centuries, in particular for writing

What does it look like?

One of 40 species in the genus *Betula*, the silver birch is a tall, deciduous tree, growing up to 30m (98ft) tall with a spread of up to 20m (66ft). That silvery bark makes it very distinctive; watch out for the deep cracks and scars in older trees. The silver birch is sometimes called the warty birch because of the odd circular protuberances on the trunk, which often look a bit like weird alien eyeballs. The leaves grow up to 6cm (2½in) long and are a shiny dark green, somewhere between oval and triangular in shape, with prominent teeth along the edges. In the autumn, the leaves turn a buttery yellow; when they fall it looks as though the tree is standing in a pool of sunshine. Catkins of both sexes grow on the same tree – the female ones green and upright, the males a little longer and drooping. The silver birch is the only one of its species that has pendulous, trailing branches. The beauty of this tree is such that the poet, Samuel Taylor Coleridge, called it "The Lady of the Woods". And, indeed, I think you'd agree that this is a very feminine tree.

sacred or magical texts. Although the bark was superseded by paper, it is still believed to be magically protective and is used to make amulets designed to keep people safe.

The birch in general has a reputation of being a guardian, perhaps because of its pioneering status, growing in places too tricky for other trees, preparing the ground physically as well as metaphorically. Babies' cradles made of birch would therefore repel the evil spirits that might otherwise steal the infant, and bundles of birch were believed to chase away malevolent entities at Halloween. And we haven't mentioned the birch rod. Although it is now against the law to hit or smack children, it wasn't very long ago that using a bundle of birch rods or just one pliable, whippy stem, was a harsh punishment for naughty boys.

The colour of silver birch, as well as its habit of peeling into strips and its connection with words and letters, opens up lots of different possibilities – that is, as long as you keep your eyes open and use your imagination! A friend of mine made something particularly inventive. Adrian found a huge piece of silver birch bark on a fallen tree. The bark came away in one large piece and he sewed up the sides with twine and turned the whole thing into a light fixture. Genius!

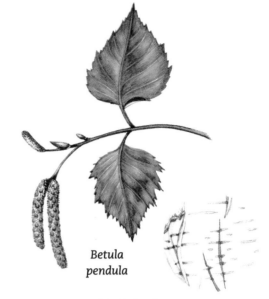

Betula pendula

Wildlife

The birch provides food and homes for over 300 species including aphids, the ladybirds that eat them and moth caterpillars. Hole-boring birds such as woodpeckers make the tree their home, and a number of birds eat the seeds.

Medicinal Uses

Traditional Western herbal medicine uses a tea made with birch leaves to dissolve kidney stones. The inner bark is used to "sweat out" a fever. Birch leaves contain phytonutrients called flavonoids, which rid the body of free radicals, therefore protecting the body from various stresses. Flavonoids are powerful antioxidants too, which are said to help the immune system resist viruses.

BIRCH BARK FIRE STARTER

If you like having bonfires in your garden, you might be interested to know that birch bark makes an incredibly efficient fire starter. It burns well even when it's wet. Next time you find a fallen birch tree, collect pieces of bark that are too small to have any other use and store then in a dry place for use when you next want to light a fire.

BIRCH WALKING STICK

I've noticed that sometimes, when I'm out walking, I find a cut stick left by some kind person in a place just where I need it, such as when I'm about to make that steep ascent. I find walking sticks really do help me stride along.

But if you'd rather not leave things to chance, why not make your own? And birch is the perfect wood to cut it from.

You need a long, straight, sturdy stick that's accessible, so that you can easily cut it down. The best branches to make a stick from are not the ones up in the tree, but the stems that you see sprouting up from the base, especially where they have been coppiced. Keep your eyes peeled and see what you can find. I like a stick with a fork at the top, so that I can grip it with my thumb.

Cut the stick to a longer length than you need, incorporating the fork (if there is one) at the top end, and then trim the bottom to the right size for your height. The easiest and safest way to cut your stick is using secateurs.

Other woods that make good walking sticks are hazel, ash, horse chestnut and cherry. One last tip. If you find a stick on the ground, make sure it is sound before you put any weight on it. Sometimes these sticks can be a bit rotten.

Blackthorn and Hawthorn

Prunus spinosa (ABOVE) and *Crataegus monogyna*
(Since these trees are often found side-by-side, planted for generations
as an impenetrable stock-proof barrier, I thought it would be a good idea
to put them together here.)

Song: "First Day of May" by Fionn Regan

Although both blackthorn and hawthorn are native to Europe and
the western part of Asia, both can also be found in eastern North
America, too. It's highly likely that the European settlers brought
these useful trees with them, either deliberately or unknowingly.
Perhaps the seeds hitched a ride in a pocket? We'll never know for
sure. Both belong, traditionally, to the fairy realms – no insipid
cartoon characters, these fairies, but a far darker type of elemental.

What does blackthorn look like?

Often seen as part of a thicket rather than as a tree, the blackthorn, left unchecked, can reach a height of 5m (16ft) with a spread of up to 6m (20ft). It has long, distinctively spiny shoots and small green leaves up to 4cm (1½in) long. The distinct dark grey-black bark gives the tree part of its name. It is easy to spot in the winter and early spring by its pretty, white, almond-scented blossoms that appear before the leaves begin to show. From midsummer onward the fruits of the blackthorn start to ripen, developing into the small stonefruits called "sloes".

While the hawthorn fairies wrap their fragrant spells around you in the spring and summer, those of the blackthorn hang around in shady places during the darker times of year, waiting to catch you on their long spiny thorns, which can give the unwary picker of sloes a nasty septic infection. So, beware!

Young sloes first appear on those spiny blackthorn bushes during early summer. They're usually missed, though, as they are tiny, bright green and hard to see in among the foliage. By autumn, sloes are dripping from the trees. Traditionally we used to wait until the first frost before harvesting them, so that the thick skins of the bitter fruits could be tamed or "bletted", by frost. The advent of the freezer might offer a short cut, but I've come to the conclusion that the nicest fruits are the naturally bletted ones. And then, of course there's sloe gin, relished by generations and subject to "best sloe gin" competitions. Have a heart for the poor judge who has been enrolled to decide which of the gleaming crimson bottles is the best. After three or more sips, any discriminatory faculties are left behind. Then, the only way to make a choice is to go for the nicest bottle!

Prunus spinosa

Crataegus monogyna

The fruits of the hawthorn – the haws – appear at any time between early summer into autumn and the colder months of the year. Although birds enjoy the fruits, I have no idea why the deep wine-red berries are often left on the trees in the winter, long after the leaves have fallen. The berries are full of pectin, the substance needed to make jams and jellies set. As for the leaves, the tender young early spring ones were, not so very long ago, nibbled by children on their way to school, certainly within living history in the UK. They were called "bread and cheese" or "bread and honey". This delightful tradition seems to have died out completely, probably because children get driven to school in cars these days. Efficient, for sure, but a shame for them to miss out on the opportunity to dawdle on the way – something that I enjoyed way too much.

Blackthorn timber grows very slowly and is incredibly dense. This quality is echoed in the Irish term "shillelagh", which means a cudgel or a club, or a piece of wood that can be used as one. A weapon made from the timber of the blackthorn tree would have been selected for its cudgel-like shape and rendered even tougher by being pushed up a chimney where it was seasoned further by soot, then polished to a boot-black lustre. Sometimes, just to make extra sure of its efficacy for bashing the enemy over the head, the cudgel would be hollowed out at the "hitting" end and molten lead was poured into the space and left to set before use. That's got to hurt.

Wildlife

The thorny tangle of blackthorn and hawthorn branches provides shelter for birds even when the leaves have dropped. Early blackthorn blossom provides welcome nectar and pollen for bees, especially during a mild spell in the winter. Hawthorn leaves are nibbled by wood mice, toads, rabbits and deer. In the winter, the tenacious hawthorn berries provide food for black bears, as well as cedar waxwings.

Medicinal Uses

Wherever sloes or hawthorn berries grow in the world they are used for medicine. Sloes are used as a cure for stomach upsets and also to ease respiratory tract ailments. Hawthorn berries treat heart conditions – among other benefits, they reduce blood pressure and can be made into a tonic to strengthen the valves of the heart.

Crataegus monogyna

What does hawthorn look like?

Hawthorn (ABOVE) reaches a height of 10m (33ft), with a similar spread and, if left to its own devices rather than being cut back as hedging, grows into quite a scruffy but beautiful tree. Like blackthorn, it also has thorny shoots. Its leaves are distinctive, cut into three or five sharply toothed lobes, glossy green on top and white or sage green underneath. Small white flowers appear after the leaves. The bark is scaly and orange-brown in colour, becoming cracked in older trees.

HAW AND SLOE FRUIT LEATHER

Since the fruits are available at roughly the same time, it makes sense to put the two together in a nutritious fruit leather.

You will need:
400g (14oz) ripe sloes
400g (14oz) ripe haws
200g (7oz) crab apples, chopped
   in half and de-pipped

100g (3½oz/1 cup) sugar, or
   to taste

1. Put the sloes and haws into a heavy-bottomed pan with enough water just to cover them, and bring to the boil. Then turn down the heat and simmer for a few minutes to help the fruits detach from the stones.

2. Leave to cool, strain out the liquid and then remove the stones – it's easy enough as the stones of both fruits are about the same size.

3. Put the liquid and the sludge left from de-stoning back into the pan and add the sugar – if you have a sweet tooth you can add a little more.

4. Simmer over a low heat, stirring so that the mixture doesn't catch on the bottom of the pan. Cook to a thick treacly consistency.

5. Line a large baking sheet with greaseproof (waxed) paper, spread the mixture as evenly as you can to a depth of no more than 3mm (⅛in). Use a second baking sheet if you have excess mixture.

6. Cook in a very low oven at about 50°C (about 120°F), with the door slightly open, for up to 8 hours. Or use a dehydrator, if you have one.

7. Once done, cut the fruit leather into strips and roll up, or use a cookie cutter and make shapes.

8. Store in a clip-top jar for up to a month.

EPINE

Epine means "thorn" or "spine" in French. This aperitif isn't made from the thorns, but from the leaves of the blackthorn tree. And it's ridiculously easy to make.

Makes 2 bottles

You will need:
2 handfuls of young
    blackthorn leaves
250ml (9fl oz/1 cup) brandy,
    or rum if you prefer
200g (7oz/1 cup) sugar

1 litre (35fl oz/4¼ cups) red
    wine, either shop-bought or
    homemade fruit wine
2 x 75cl (26fl oz) glass bottles

1. Simply put all the ingredients into a large food-grade container with a lid, and leave for a couple of weeks, stirring occasionally.
2. Strain through a jelly bag or similar, and bottle.
3. Serve chilled over ice, or as a hot cocktail by adding ginger, peppercorns and a couple of slices of pear.

SLOE GIN

If you want to make a really good sloe gin, go easy on the sugar. Half fill a 70cl (26fl oz) bottle with cleaned and bletted fresh or frozen sloes, fill to within 6cm (2½in) of the top of the bottle with either gin or vodka, and then add just a couple of teaspoonfuls of sugar. Leave for a few weeks, shaking from time to time, then taste; if you feel you need it sweeter, simply add sweetening to taste.

Usually made in the late autumn and ready to drink by Christmas, sloe gin is better consumed in February, when you need cheering up.

Cedar

Cedrus libani

Song: "Norwegian Wood" by The Beatles

Here's a question for you. How does the cedar link together the following: Hindu gods, ancient Egyptian embalming practices, writing and the American naturalist, Henry Thoreau? In this list I could include the churchyard in my village, which contains several unexpectedly grand trees, including three beautiful cedars. It's a long way from home for these trees, which have their origins in the Lebanon, the Himalayas and Pakistan. These particular trees were probably gifted to the church by someone wealthy enough to be able to afford such lovely specimens. But I'll never know for sure.

Here are the answers. The etymology of the deodar cedar (*Cedrus deodara*) is particularly interesting. In Sanskrit, the name translates as *deva daru*. *Deva* means "divine", also an attribute of the Hindu pantheon, and *daru* is "tree". *Daru* is also linked to the words "druid", "true" and "tree".

Cedarwood oil from the cedar of Lebanon is an effective insect repellent and so was used for this property by embalmers in ancient Egypt to keep the corpse clear of insects and bugs while it was being worked on. The oil was also injected into the bodily cavities to dissolve the soft organs. The association with death might well be why cedar trees are often found in cemeteries and graveyards, including in my village.

Cedarwood also traditionally gives us a common and useful everyday item – the pencil. Cheap and abundant, pencils last for ages, and one of the best things about them is that they need sharpening once in a while. Probably like you, I'm a bit of a stationery freak, and have a number of different pencil sharpening devices. The best part of sharpening a pencil is the deeply satisfying aroma of the paper-thin wood shavings as you carefully try to make the curling spiral as long as you can before it breaks.

The delightful sensory thrill of pencil shavings is all due to the fragrant softwood that encases the graphite. The wood first used was actually a juniper (*Juniperus virginiana*, also called the pencil cedar), but this has since been superseded by the incense cedar, a true cedar. And the wood of this cedar tree is said to make the most fragrant pencils of all.

The answer to the last question is a little longer. What follows is part of the story of an influential, and very interesting, naturalist. Henry David Thoreau was born in Massachusetts in 1817. I'd love to have met him. Thoreau was a great thinker whose ideas are even more valid now than when he was alive. It seems there was nothing that Thoreau, a natural philosopher, wasn't interested in – poetry, religion, politics, biology, history and politics, as well as all aspects of the natural world, jostled for space in his brilliant mind. Thoreau also believed that humans are as much a part of the natural world as any other creature and that we should be able to live simply and harmoniously with nature.

He didn't just talk about these ideals in his book *Walden, or Life in the Forest*, he lived by them too. In 1848, he set out to see how far he could take the experiment in simple living by building himself a small hut on land lent to him by his friend, the writer Ralph Waldo Emerson. He turned the "normal" way of working upside down, showing that it was possible to work for just one day a week if you live a frugal life, therefore freeing yourself for the rest of the time to follow your own path. Thoreau used

Cedrus libani

What does it look like?

There are several different cedars, which are part of the pine family, Pinaceae, and here I've used the cedar of Lebanon (*Cedrus libani*) as an example. Growing to a height of 30m (98ft) with a spread of 20m (66ft), this cedar, like all the others, is evergreen. The bark is dark grey, cracking into little squares with age. The needle-like leaves are also dark green-grey, 3cm (1¼in) long, carried singly on long shoots and in thick whorls on shorter side shoots. In time, the cedar attains its characteristic broad, flat-topped canopy and "stepped" branches. It has upright male cones, 5cm (2in) long, dotted along the branches.

that free time well – writing, walking, thinking, growing vegetables, observing nature and generally being a living demonstration of what could be possible for humankind.

His father owned a failing pencil factory, and it was here that he spent his one day per week working. Becoming obsessed with pencils, he made a point of finding out everything he could about the superior ones being made in Europe, and so improved the Thoreau pencil that it became America's leading writing tool, dominating the market. It was the cedarwood pencil he perfected that paid for the publication of *Walden*.

The themes that Thoreau espouses – personal responsibility, simple living on the land in harmony with nature, sustainability – are so much a part of our lives right now. I can't tell you here how to make your own pencils, but I can offer you a slightly left-field use for cedarwood oil and something that I think Thoreau would have loved, as he was an avid letter-writer.

Wildlife
The cracks and crevices common to an ageing cedar provide perfect nesting places and shelter for birds such as tawny owls. Bats also roost in the branches.

Medicinal Uses
Considered trees of the gods in India for their application in ayurvedic medicine, various cedars were used to treat ailments including rheumatism, piles, fevers, pulmonary and urinary disorders, bruising, skin diseases, joint pain and more.

CEDARWOOD INCENSE AND SCENTED PAPER
If you like burning joss sticks, you will love making your own. You can use any essential oil that you wish, but here I'm using cedarwood oil. Despite the name, this is usually a mixture of oils

from different types of conifer trees including juniper and cyprus, as well as cedar. It all smells lovely.

You will need:
10 or more "blank" joss sticks (easy to buy from specialist stores online)
Cedarwood essential oil

Good-quality, naturally absorbent paper, such as cartridge paper.

1. Find a shallow glass or china container a little longer than your joss stick blanks. I use a long olive dish.
2. Pour enough essential oil into the dish for up to 10 joss sticks to be in contact with it.
3. Cover, and leave for a couple of days.
4. Lift out the joss sticks one at a time and let excess oil drip away.
5. Lay the sticks on the cartridge paper to dry out for a day or so before burning.
6. Cut the cartridge paper into small strips and pop a strip into the envelope of a letter to a loved one or a friend as a fragrant treat.

PENCIL SHARPENING THE OLD-FASHIONED WAY

Rarely witnessed these days, sharpening a fragrant cedarwood pencil with a knife is an art worth mastering, even if only for the satisfaction of a nice sharp point and the endeavour's retro aspect!

First, make sure your knife is really sharp; a pocket knife or a pen knife is fine, sharpened if necessary with a kitchen sharpener or, failing that, on a kerbstone.

Always push the knife away from you. Angle the knife along the flat side of the pencil and shave smoothly and carefully, one side at a time. Don't worry about speed – concentrate on finding the correct pressure. Take great care when using the knife and if you are unfamiliar with using knives in this way, find someone to help you.

Cherry

Prunus avium

Song: "Black Horse and the Cherry Tree" by KT Tunstall

As I'm writing this on an early autumn morning, I'm lucky enough to be looking out of my window at a small cherry tree, planted almost five years ago. The birds got most of the fruits a few weeks ago, but right now I'm seeing something even better – the autumn leaves. Before they fall, cherry leaves give out a spectacular firework display of colourful foliage, ranging through a spectrum of pale reds, pinks, shades of yellow and orange and even a crazy salmon pink that only a cherry tree can get away with. It's quite psychedelic – nature's lava lamp. The word "cherry" also borrows from the name of the colour "cerise" – from the French and derived from the Latin *cerasum* – a deep pinky-red hue that cheers the soul on a drab day.

The fruit of the tree, the cherry itself, contains a stone. This means that in botanical terms the cherry is a drupe, like the peach, the plum, the olive – and even the mango.

In Japan, the annual return of the cherry blossoms attracts visitors from all over the world. This celebration is not just a visual feast, but a spiritual one, too. Shinto and Buddhism, the two main religions in the country, both perceive the brief but glorious appearance of the blossoms as symbolic of our own short lives. Shinto is particularly appealing to the nature-lover, an ancient

What does it look like?

The wild cherry, also called the gean, is deciduous and grows to a height of 25m (82ft) with a spread of 15m (49ft). The bark is very distinctive, horizontally striped, glossy red-brown, peeling into strips on older trees. The tree flowers profusely in spring, and the shiny red fruits appear on long stalks from late spring to summer and into autumn. Leaves are up to 15cm (6in) long, oval to kite-shaped, with tiny saw-like teeth.

There are hundreds of different varieties of cherry, all believed to have descended from the original trees that grew in Greece and Turkey. There's another wild cherry variety, too, worth mentioning: the bird cherry (*Prunus padus*). This cherry tree is common and likely to attract you by its lovely honeyed scent in the spring, but its fruits don't grow in the same way as a "normal" cherry. Bird cherries have long clusters of flowers followed by equally long clusters of small fruits, which birds go crazy for. If you were able to get to the small fruits before the birds, you'd find that they are unpalatably sour (although a sour cherry is the best kind for making cherry brandy – equal parts of sherry, sugar and brandy).

polytheistic belief system that revolves around the supernatural spirits that inhabit all things. This idea is reflected in Sufism, too. There's a wonderful saying to the effect that every drop of dew and blade of grass has a spirit that is sacred. I like this idea. We can't be certain there's a heaven or a hell, but we can appreciate where we are and put ourselves into the moment.

Prunus avium

Wildlife

Spring flowers are a much-needed source of pollen and nectar for bees. The cherries are eaten by several bird species, including the song thrush and the blackbird, as well as mice and badgers. Cherry leaves are a primary source of food for several moth caterpillars, including the cherry bark moth and the short-cloaked moth.

Medicinal Uses

Up until World War II, cherry stalks of any species were used for patients with anaemia, loose bowels or bronchitis. The stalks were simply infused for a time and then administered by mouth. This medicine has not yet been tested. The black cherry (*Prunus serotina*) has been used as a tonic medicine for a long time, certainly before we knew that the deep red skins of the fruit contain anthocyanins, which have immune-boosting antiviral and antibacterial properties.

FERMENTED CHERRIES

Fermented fruits and vegetable are great at keeping our gut bacteria healthy. You can use these savoury cherries on a pizza, as well as with a cheeseboard or in a cocktail.

You will need:

2kg (4lb 8oz) fresh cherries

1½ tbsp sea salt

A wide-mouthed glass jar with a clip top

1. Remove the stems and any debris, and pit the cherries into a bowl, using a sharp knife or a de-stoning gadget. Throw away any badly damaged fruit.
2. Toss the cherries in the salt, squeezing them slightly. Add 250ml (9fl oz/1 cup) of water.
3. Put all ingredients into the jar, ensuring the fruits are submerged.
4. Ferment at room temperature for a couple of days and then transfer to the fridge to slow down the fermentation process.
5. After the cherries are eaten, use the liquid as a sourdough starter.

CHERRY BLOSSOM AND LIME SYRUP

This is a lovely way to prolong the short cherry blossom season. Use drizzled onto ice cream, diluted with sparkling water, or in a cocktail.
Makes about 500ml (17fl oz)

You will need:

1 mug (300ml/10½fl oz/1¼ cups in volume) freshly gathered cherry blossoms, unwashed

200g (7oz/1 cup) sugar

Juice of 1 lime

A 500ml (17fl oz) glass bottle, sterilized

1. Put the blossoms in a pan and add 300ml (10½fl oz/1¼ cups) water.
2. Bring to the boil, then turn off the heat and allow the petals to infuse for 4 hours.
3. Strain away the petals, giving them a squeeze, and add the sugar.
4. Bring to the boil again and cook until reduced by just over a half.
5. Leave to cool, then add the lime juice.
6. Strain into the bottle and store in a cool place.

Christmas Tree

Pinus (ABOVE LEFT), *Abies, Picea*

**Song: Tchaikovsky's "Nutcracker Suite", no. 8
(Scene in a Pine Forest)**

The first Christmas tree in the UK is said to have been introduced by Prince Albert, the German consort of Queen Victoria, in 1846. Although it's generally thought that the well-heeled East Coast American Society adopted the practice in the US, German settlers had been bringing trees and greenery into their homes for quite some time before Prince Albert legitimized an ancient pagan custom. The custom had been not without controversy. In the UK, Oliver Cromwell (notorious for several reasons, including cancelling

Christmas altogether from 1644 to 1660, which is such an outrageous concept that people are still talking about it) said that singing carols and decorating trees was a "heathen tradition". In 1659 the Plymouth Colony tried to put a stop to the "pagan mockery" of Christmas trees, and in the same joyless year, the General Court of Massachusetts declared any sort of celebration, apart from a church service, would see revellers put in prison. Why would such a pleasant, innocent symbol of light be the focus of so much fraught attention? Here's my theory.

Abies alba

There seems to be tension between religious ideals and the natural world, based on the irrational idea that both can't exist in harmony with one another. It's no wonder so many fairy tales are set in dense coniferous forests, which are easy to get lost in – unsafe places, unknown, dangerous, full of talking animals. To let a little of a forest into your home is to bring in something of that danger, but tamed, on your terms: a meeting of the darkness and the light. And yet, being in a forest is not only an education but a delight that borders on the spiritual, calming our souls and clearing our minds.

Picea abies

As it happens, pine, spruce and fir are all edible. This is a secret known to many Native American people. However, if you have

Pseudotsuga menziesii

bought a (real) tree from most commercial enterprises, be aware that chemicals are often sprayed onto the trees, mainly to make them last longer. Best not eat this kind. And by the way, although pine-type scents are often used in household cleaning products, the scent of the actual trees neither tastes nor smells of toilet cleaner. Hope this helps.

Wildlife

The Douglas fir (*Pseudotsuga menziesii*) provides important shelter for rare red squirrels and pine martens. Home to hover flies, weevils and beetles, the Norway spruce (*Picea abies*) offers its foliage as food for the carpet moth. Red squirrels eat the cones. The woody cones of pine trees contain nutritious seeds that feed all manner of birds, as well as squirrels and other mammals, including humans. If you've ever eaten pine nuts, you can thank the stone pine (*Pinus pinea*) for them.

Medicinal Uses

Pine trees yield oil of turpentine, which has had a number of uses, including as a stimulant applied topically to aching joints. There are many different pines with various medicinal uses. For example, the volatile oil found in spruce is rich in terpenes, which have antiseptic and antibacterial qualities. Black spruce contains monoterpenes, which make it helpful for respiratory issues. Balsam fir resin is used by the First Nations (specifically, the Penobscot of the Maine area) as an antiseptic for cuts and wounds; indeed, the sap has been found to be antiseptic and does indeed have pain-relieving qualities. For all the benefits of these trees, there are also many unsubstantiated claims about them, including a suggestion that pine-pollen has anti-ageing properties. However adding pine oil extract to a hot bath helps relieve muscular tension and the aroma is just wonderful.

What does it look like?

Is it a pine, a fir or a spruce? All the trees liable to be used as a traditional Christmas tree fall into the category of pine (*Pinus*), fir (*Abies*) or spruce (*Picea*). And all three trees are conifers, meaning that they produce cones. Although we tend to think of pinecones as a generic term for all cones, this is wrong. Pine trees have pinecones, fir trees have fir cones, and spruce trees ... you get the idea!

Just as deciduous trees can be identified by their leaves so, too, can the pine, fir or spruce. In fact, it's easier to identify conifers because their needle-shaped leaves stay on the tree all year round. Use the comparisons between each tree to work out which is which. The following is all about the sense of touch; try closing your eyes when feeling the textures of these needles.

- Pine: The needles are arranged, and attached to the branches, in clusters of two, three, or five needles per cluster. Whether open or closed, pinecones feel rigid rather than flexible.

- Spruce: Needles are attached individually to the branches. If you're wearing gloves, take them off and pluck a needle. It will be sharply pointed with a square profile, easy to roll between your fingers. Spruce needles are attached to small, stalk-like woody lumps. When the needles fall, these lumpy projections remain behind, leaving a rough texture to the branches. The cones of a spruce hang down from the branches, with narrow scales that feel flexible.

- Fir: Despite their sharp tips, fir needles are softer, flat and not easy to roll between your fingers, unlike the spruce. Since they don't have the same lumpy projections, you will feel that the bark is smooth. The cones stand upright high up in the branches and often break as they fall. If you know of a forested area, watch out for fallen trees to access cones from the even the highest trees.

Let's put this all into shorthand.
- Pine: two, three or five needles; hard, woody cones.
- Spruce: sharp, pointed needle can be rolled between your fingers; rough-textured bark.
- Fir: soft flat needles, not easy to roll; smooth bark.

CHRISTMAS TREE TEA

This needle tea, made by Native Americans, is packed full of vitamin C and just the thing to boost your immune system.

Makes 2 large cups

You will need:

2 tbsp fir, pine or spruce needles, either fresh or dried, slightly crushed

1 cinnamon stick

6 cardamom pods, lightly crushed

A thumb-sized chunk of ginger, shredded

A few strips of unwaxed citrus zest of your choice

Honey, to taste

A 2-litre (70fl oz) glass jar, to allow flavours to develop

1. Place all the ingredients apart from the honey into the jar and leave for a couple of days, to let the different scents get acquainted.
2. Warm a teapot by swishing hot water around it, then put a heaped teaspoon of the pine mixture per person into the pot, pour over freshly boiled water and steep for about 8 minutes.
3. Pour into cups and add honey to taste.

CHRISTMAS TREE MASSAGE OIL

Collect enough sprigs of pine, spruce or fir to fill a clean jam jar. Remove any debris, pop the sprigs into the jar and cover with a neutral oil, such as sunflower oil. Allow to infuse for a few weeks, then strain out the solids by putting a fine-meshed sieve over a jug. This straining process may take some time – overnight or longer. Strain the oil a second time, this time through muslin (cheesecloth). Apply slightly warmed oil to aching joints or use as a massage oil.

VIKING WHISK (TVARE OR QUIRL)

This handy utensil was used by Vikings back in the 9th century. You can make them as long or as short as you fancy – long for stirring the contents of a bubbling cauldron outdoors, or a more normal size for daily use. The best time to harvest the top of a Christmas tree is just after everyone has taken them down, when you'll see a lot of easily accessible discarded trees. I like the idea that we are making something from them rather than throwing them away.

You will need:

The stem and first layer of branches from the top of a used Christmas tree

A sharp whittling knife
Sandpaper in different grades, if necessary

1. First, cut off the part of the tree that you need: the long central stem and the layer of branches stretched out below it.
2. Remove the needles and bark, revealing the smooth, white wood.
3. If the layer of branches is uneven or pointing in different directions, tie them close to the stem, pop them into hot water overnight and leave to dry for a day or so.
4. Cut the branches to length and gently even them out.
5. You now have your whisk: a handle with about 5 tines pointing back toward the stem.

Elder

Sambucus nigra

Song: "Magic Tree" by Ruu Campbell

Varieties of elder trees abound, and the tree can be found not only in Europe but also in the Himalayas, Canada, the USA, Africa, Asia, and elsewhere. It grows prolifically in hedgerows and at the edge of woods or forests as a stand-alone tree or as a shrub. During winter, it looks like a scruffy bundle of sticks. In spring, however, the Cinderella that is the elder tree transforms into a beauty, covered in loose clusters of creamy flowers, each blossom no bigger than the end of a matchstick. On a hot day, the scent is the absolute definition of summer. It's the blossoms that are used to make

What does it look like?

Elder grows naturally to a height of 10m (33ft), with a spread of 8m (26ft). Its shape is generally quite shrubby, with lots of stems emerging from the base of the tree. The bark is grey-brown, smooth initially, developing grooved fissures with age. Leaves (which smell quite acrid if you squeeze and sniff them) are pinnate, with five to seven pairs of leaflets up to 20cm (8in) in length sitting opposite one another along the stem, with an "extra" leaf at the end. By early summer the buds transform into the distinctive flat-topped umbels (flower clusters) of elderflowers, followed a few weeks later by the drooping bundles of red-stemmed, glistening black berries. Incidentally, the jelly ear fungus (*Auricularia auricula judae*) grows most commonly on elder wood.

elderflower cordial and champagne, both easy to make and well worth doing. Then the petals fall away. Observant people will notice tiny green dots emerging from where the centre of the blossoms used to be. Throughout summer and into early autumn these little green sparks get larger and larger, graduating from green to shiny black, forming in clusters like the flowers. Where the blossoms turn their faces up to the sun, though, these glittering, blue-black droplets of goodness are much heavier and weigh down the branches.

There's no doubt that the elder has a witchy reputation. In Europe, for thousands of years, people believed that the tree was inhabited by a female spirit, the Elder Mother, whom you might think of as a very strict but fair teacher, very kind and benevolent but also quick to anger. The tree was treated with the respect accorded by such a reputation, including an invocation that people gave if they needed to cut an elder. The words were: "*Lady Ellhorn, give me some of thy woodland and I will give thee some of mine when it grows in the forest*". There's also a long tradition of the tree being protective, hence elder branches were nailed outside homes to keep the witches away.

And there are the usual contradictions common to folk magic – for example, although witches are said to gather wherever the trees are full of fruit, a wand made of elder is also said to ward off evil spirits.

Elder's Latin name – *Sambucus* – comes from *sambuke*, the Greek word for

Sambucus nigra

a stringed instrument a bit like a lyre. It's possible that elder wood was once used to make the body of this instrument. There's a pan-pipe type of woodwind instrument, too, with the same name, originally made from the hollow stems of the tree.

Probably the best-known use of the *sambuca*, though, is the delicious liqueur made from elderberries and anise. This is the drink that comes in a shot glass with a coffee bean on the top. The waiter sets it on fire, and you blow out the flames to release the oils in the coffee bean.

Wildlife

Various insects feed on elderflower nectar, and the berries are enjoyed by many birds. Dormice and voles consume both the flowers and the berries. The foliage is eaten by moth caterpillars including the swallow-tailed, the buff ermine and the dot moth.

Medicinal Uses

Elder offers a veritable cabinet of first-aid remedies, way beyond the remit of this book. Many of the efficacies attributed to it are traditional remedies, but the plant has also undergone medical trials for its antioxidant and anthocyanin qualities. Leaves can form the basis of green elder ointment, which is used for treating chilblains, sprains and bruises. Elderflower water, made from the dried flowers, is good for making eye and skin lotions – soak cotton wool with it and apply to ease conjunctivitis or screen-weary eyes. Elderflowers are also startlingly handy for hayfever sufferers. Simply infuse the flowers in cold water for a few hours and drink as needed. The anthocyanins in elderberries, mentioned above, contain antioxidants, which are used in the treatment of cancer. They are also full of phytochemicals that are not only antiviral but also boost the immune system. And as a cure for colds and flu, elderberry has no rival.

MAKE AN ELDER WHISTLE OR BEADS

An interesting quirk about elder wood is that the pith can easily be pushed out of the stems, leaving a hollow tube. This is why it is also called "pipe tree" or "bore tree". It's very easy to cut (with permission, of course) a thickish stem of elder, then push out the pith with a knitting needle or similar and turn the hollow stem into a whistle by adding a slim sliver of the wood into the bottom of the tube. You can also make beads in the same way. Find a decent-sized stem, cut between the nodes, push out the pith and carefully slice the hollow tube to make beads to your own specification. You could even carve magical symbols onto the beads.

ELDERBERRY WINTER TONIC

This tonic works. You can buy an over-the-counter version but making your own renders it much more efficacious because you will have put your time and effort into it, as well as made a profound connection with the tree. And you'll also have had a nice time out in the open collecting the berries, preferably with a dog for company.
Makes about 1 litre (35fl oz)

You will need:

20 bunches of elderberries, stripped from their stalks

250g (9oz/scant 1 cup) molasses

1 unwaxed lemon, chopped into 8 pieces

1 cinnamon stick

A 4cm (2in) chunk of ginger, chopped into 8 pieces

1 tbsp ground turmeric

A few cloves

Black pepper

A 1-litre (35fl oz) glass bottle

1. Put the berries in a heavy pan, adding enough water to cover. Put the lid on and bring to a boil, letting it boil for 3 or 4 minutes.
2. Allow to cool, then strain the liquid through a wire-meshed sieve. You will find there's quite a bit of thick "juice" left in the sieve that can be pushed through with the back of a spoon and a little effort.
3. Put the strained liquid back into the pan and add the rest of the ingredients. Give it a good stir.
4. Cover the pan and bring slowly to a simmer. Allow to simmer, without boiling, for about 30 minutes.
5. Turn off the heat but leave the pan with the lid on for a few hours until completely cold, then bottle.
6. Drink neat or mix with water, as you prefer. Can also be poured over porridge or yoghurt.

PONTACK SAUCE

This is an ancient recipe, once used with gamey meats such as venison. It's a sort of medieval ketchup, said to be at its best after seven years, but it's unlikely you'll want to wait that long to try it!

Makes about 1 litre (35fl oz)

You will need:

500g (1lb 2oz) elderberries, stripped from the stalks

250ml (9fl oz/1 cup) cider vinegar

A 4cm (2in) chunk of ginger, bruised

10 shallots, peeled and thinly sliced

6 cloves

4 allspice berries

1 blade of mace

1 tbsp whole black peppercorns (not cracked)

A 1-litre (35fl oz) glass bottle, sterilized

1. Put the berries and the vinegar into an enamel or glass ovenproof dish and cook in a low oven for 4 hours.

2. Once cooked, leave the berries and vinegar to cool, then sieve, using the back of a spoon to squeeze as much of the elderberry through as you can.

3. Put the juice back into the pan and add all the other ingredients. Bring to a gentle boil and cook for about 30 minutes until the liquid has reduced by about one-fifth (you'll see a tide mark on the pan).

4. Allow to cool, then sieve again. This will make the sauce smoother.

5. Return the liquid to the pan and boil for 5 minutes.

6. Allow to cool, then pour into the bottle, and store in a cool place.

You could eat this as an accompaniment to game meats, as Henry VIII of England did, or just as easily use it as a dip for your fries.

Fig

Ficus carica

Song: "Banyan Tree" by Machine Gun Kelly

One of the best-known stories about the fig tree is how Adam and Eve, having eaten the forbidden fruit from the Tree of Knowledge, realize that they are naked, and make use of the handily sized leaves of the fig tree to cover their modesty. Fig leaves tend to be quite large and are also relatively smooth to the touch. It's also fortunate for Adam and Eve that this biblical story didn't take place in, say, Scandinavia, where, with all those pine forests, there is nowhere to hide, it's rather chilly and the pine needles are uncomfortably prickly.

Fig 65

Fig trees are widespread throughout the Mediterranean countries, as well as in India, and have naturalized in many other parts of the world, including the USA, the rest of Europe and the UK. Where the climate tends toward being temperate, the tree needs to be protected from cold and frost. The fig is inclined to bear fruit more readily if its roots are restricted. I have two figs in pots in my garden, which were fairly unceremoniously pulled up, shoved into a plastic bag and then driven across the country on a boiling hot day – and then even further neglected by being left in the car. When I eventually remembered them, they looked pretty dead, but I planted them all together in a large pot and forgot all about them again. Then, in the autumn, I discovered that they seemed to be thriving, despite such rough treatment. And they are still alive today and doing nicely.

The fig is a salutary reminder of just how resilient a plant can be. Not far from where I live is Blaenavon, an old coal mining town that has a unique industrial heritage: the site of the world's first iron mines. It has been designated a UNESCO World Heritage site, right up there with the Great Wall of China and the pyramids in Egypt. I was taking a group of people on a foraging walk there a while ago, past an old bridge and a tumbledown building. One of them suddenly stopped, pointed and asked "What's that plant? It looks like a fig tree!" My first thought was that he must be mistaken – but he was right. This part of the world is notoriously cold and wet, with long winters when the temperature drops below freezing on a regular basis. The fig tree was growing from the arched part of the bridge and sprawled across the front wall of the building with not much shelter. What's more, the ground beneath was covered in sticky splatters of overripe fruit, thousands of tiny seeds clear to see, but the fruit, annoyingly, was out of our reach.

The walk ground to a halt as we tried to work out how on earth the fig tree had got there in the first place. Had it been planted deliberately? Or carried by a bird? How was it pollinated?

Of course, we'll never know, but I just couldn't stop speculating how this fig had found itself in such an unlikely place.

The last coal mines in Blaenavon closed in February 1990, amid conflicting emotions for the community. Although the work was tough, it was nevertheless part of local tradition dating back centuries. As soon as the ironworks had opened in 1789, the population had shot up rapidly as people came to find work, not just from the UK, but from Russia, Poland, France – and Spain, a Mediterranean country where figs come from. A fig tree can live for two hundred years, so it was possible that this particular one could have been brought as a fruit, all the way from Spain to Blaenavon. Perhaps – just perhaps – a young man called, say, Matias, had arrived in Blaenavon with the intention of sending riches back to his mama in, say, Seville. And perhaps Mama had put the fig in his pocket to remind him of home. One day, perhaps on a Sunday after church (the only day that Matias would have had free), he walked to

Ficus carica

the bridge and sat on it, looking across the valley ravaged by mines, fires relentlessly blazing into the skies. He would have been feeling sad. What if he put his hand in his pocket, found the fig and wept for his lost family, wondering if he would ever make it home? By now, the fig would have been quite old, covered in fluff and grime and definitely no longer edible. What if Matias crushed what was left of it into the crack of the bridge, which would have been quite new at that time? What do you think? Plausible?

Fig 67

The thing is that we'll never know. But it's fun to make up a story, especially if you can marry it up with the facts that you do know, to make it seem more likely. And that is often what foraging is all about. Most of the plants you think of as being cultivated were certainly wild in the first place.

Wildlife

Uniquely, the flower of the fig is found on the inside of the fruit and is pollinated by the female fig wasp, which burrows into the fig and lays her eggs inside the flowers, at the same time transferring pollen from the fig she previously visited. The tree then realizes that there's an egg and surrounds it with plant tissue. The fig wasp flies further than any other pollinator, more than 10km (6 miles). The plant is

What does it look like?

There are many species of fig, but our example here is the common fig. Deciduous, with a spreading habit, the common fig reaches a height and spread of around 10m (33ft). It has a shrubby appearance, with some branches growing quite low down. The bark is pale grey and smooth. The leaves of a fig are unusual: deeply lobed, glossy green above and a little rough, with hairs. The flowers are tiny, with females and males on separate plants, which are carried on the inside of the structure that becomes the fruit. In the autumn, the hard, green, teardrop-shaped figs ripen to a rich purple-brown colour. The fig itself isn't a fruit, but a capsule of inverted micro-flowers called an "inflorescence". Each delicious fruit, which can be eaten whole – skin and all – contains thousands of tiny seeds. Moreover, the fig tree can produce fruit all year round. It is also used in re-forestation of the rain forest.

known as a "keystone species" with over 1,300 different creatures relying on it, including other wasps, bees and birds, which all relish the ripe fruits, whether these are hanging on the trees or squashed on the ground.

Medicinal Uses

The main medicinal use for fig fruits seems to be universally known! They have been used as an effective laxative for generations – syrup of figs, if the problem isn't too bad, and the stronger compound of syrup of figs in an emergency. The latter medicine is further fortified by rhubarb and senna.

FRESH RIPE FIGS

Quite honestly, if you have a load of fresh ripe figs, you can probably do no better than to cut them in half, grill (broil) them until soft and slightly scorched, then drizzle them with honey and add a dollop of Greek yoghurt.

FIGGY FANCY DRESS

This is a suggestion that you're unlikely to find in any other book about trees.

Next time you find a fig leaf, carry it home and look after it until such a time as you are invited to a fancy-dress party (or, if there are no parties on the horizon, you simply feel like startling the neighbours).

Then, find or purchase a vest top and some leggings to match your skin colour as closely as possible and simply attach the leaf to the appropriate place, paying due care and attention to the safety pins.

Voilà! All you need now to complete the outfit is an apple and a boa constrictor.

Fig 69

Guelder Rose

Viburnum opulus

**Song: "All the Trees of the Field Will Clap Their Hands"
by Sufjan Stevens**

The "guelder" part of this tree's name refers to Gueldersland in
the Netherlands, where the plant is believed to have originated.
In the USA, one of the names for its berries is "European cranberries",
which is a nod to the "real" cranberry that the berries can resemble.
As well as growing in the USA and other parts of the world, it is
prolific in Russia, the Ukraine, Romania and other Slavic countries,
where the mythology of this unique little tree is closely interrelated.
The bright, rich red of the berries – which are called *kalina* –
symbolize beauty, love and passion.

You might have heard the song, "Kalinka", which is the diminutive version of *kalina*. It starts in a very stately way, quite slowly, but gradually gathers pace like a runaway train. The dance that accompanies the song gets faster and faster too, until it comes to a halt with a huge flourish. "Kalinka" means "little berry" and refers to the guelder rose as the "snowberry":

Little snowberry, snowberry, snowberry of mine!
Little raspberry in the garden, my little raspberry!

Ah, under the pine, the green one,
Lay me down to sleep,
Rock-a-bye, baby, rock-a-bye, baby,
Lay me down to sleep.

Little snowberry, snowberry, snowberry of mine!
Little raspberry in the garden, my little raspberry!

Ah, little pine, little green one,
Don't rustle above me.

I find this little tree quite cheeky, a bit of a shapeshifter and somewhat deceptive, although innocently so. I really can't imagine that a tree would be deliberately misleading, but who knows? Here are my reasonings.

- The guelder rose is quite common, although many people don't know its name.
- The glittering brightness of the berries, for some, is taken as a warning sign that they must be toxic – but they're not.
- Because the leaves are quite unusual and difficult to place, the tree is often mistaken for some sort of maple, which it's not.
- As mentioned above, the fluffy blossoms might look a bit like elderflowers, but their scent is totally different.

- Once the leaves have shrivelled away and the berries have been snaffled by blackbirds, the tree can go back to being virtually unnoticed.
- And finally, the berries, when squished, sometimes smell a bit like vomit. When cooked, they smell similarly icky. But when the berries are made into a jelly or jam, both the scent and the odour are pleasantly fragrant and floral, and well worth a try. Just warn anyone else who might be in the house.

Viburnum opulus

What does it look like?

This is a relatively small, sprawling tree, growing to a height of 4–5m (13–16ft) and with a similar spread. The bark is a greyish brown, and the branches are tangled up like loose knitting. The flowers, which appear from spring onward, are gorgeous – flat-topped and creamy white, with a circle of larger blossoms protecting the smaller ones in the centre. To the untrained eye they could be mistaken for elder flowers, but the differing sizes of the flowers, as well as the scent and the leaf-shape, help with recognition. Guelder rose leaves are very pretty, similar to those of a maple (see page 101). They are up to 8cm (3¼in) long, with three to five irregular lobes. The berries, which are a clear, bright red, appear from midsummer onward. In early autumn, the entire tree blazes red and is a really cheery sight in the hedgerows.

Wildlife

Birds, especially the mistle thrush and the bullfinch, love guelder rose berries, and you'll often see spatters of white droppings on the branches of the tree when it is in fruit. Hoverflies love the flowers, too.

Medicinal Uses

An ancient name for this tree is "cramp bark", which gives a pretty good clue that the bark is effective in relieving cramps. Specifically, it's used to relax the muscles of the uterus and is therefore helpful for a number of gynecological conditions, including period pain. The use of guelder rose seems to be universal throughout Europe, North America and northern Asia. It's fascinating how different peoples, living far apart from one another, often use the same plants for the same reasons. The active ingredient is a coumarin derivative called scopoletin, which contains volatile oils that relax uterine cramps, making them less painful. As well as this, guelder rose bark contains a compound, methyl salicylate, that has similar properties to aspirin.

GUELDER ROSE JELLY
Makes 4 jars

You will need:

800g (1lb 12oz) soft, ripe guelder rose berries

2 small oranges, peeled and chopped

12 crab apples, for pectin

White granulated sugar (quantity varies, see method overleaf)

A squeeze of lemon juice

4 x 300ml (10½fl oz) glass jars, sterilized

1. Put all the ingredients except the sugar and the lemon juice into a heavy-bottomed pan with 500ml (17fl oz/2 cups) water and bring to a simmer. Cook for 15 minutes, occasionally mashing the contents.

2. Cool, and strain overnight using a jelly bag or muslin cloth (cheesecloth). Don't squeeze, otherwise your jelly will be cloudy.

3. Pour the liquid into a measuring jug and for every 100ml (3½fl oz/ scant ½ cup) liquid, add 100g (3½oz/½ cup) sugar.

4. Heat the mixture gently, stirring all the while so that the sugar dissolves. Add the lemon juice.

5. Simmer for 20 minutes, until setting point is reached. You can use a sugar thermometer if you have one – it will need reach 105°C (221°F). If not, use the cold saucer method. Put a saucer in the fridge for an hour or so, then when you think the jelly is ready, take it out and drop a blob on the saucer. Leave for half a minute or so, then tilt the saucer. If the jelly sets on the saucer, then it is ready.

6. As the jelly cools a little, sterilize your jars and dry with a hot tea towel or in a low oven.

7. Pour the jelly into the jars, leave until cold, then put the lids on.

FEED THE BIRDS

A bird will lose a substantial proportion of its body weight during one cold winter's night, and unless it is able to replenish its reserves, a prolonged cold spell can often be catastrophic. Given that birds adore the sparkly red berries of the guelder rose, my suggestion here is very simple. Gather a few bunches from trees wherever you see the berries, strip them from the stalks and freeze them until winter when the birds need all the sustenance they can find.

If you have one, a bird table can make a huge difference to improving birds' chances of survival through very cold periods. Put out your frozen guelder berries and, if you can, provide other regular food for them, such as meal worms, fat-balls, crushed peanuts, dried fruit, seeds and grain. You will be doing them a great service.

Hazel

Corylus avellana

Song: "Ragged Wood" by Fleet Foxes

The word "hazel" derives from the Anglo-Saxon *haesel* meaning "hat", hence *haesel knut*, means "a nut wearing a hat". If you look at a hazel nut, which has a pair of frilly flaps around its edge a bit like a trapper's hat, you'll see just how appropriate this descriptive name is.

Despite its cheerful modesty, the hazel played a vital role in the lives of our ancestors. After the Ice Age, the first tree to emerge was the birch, and following close behind, colonizing the bare earth and enriching it for other plants to thrive, was the hazel. As taller trees came along, the hazel was pushed to the edges of the forests, where it wasn't shaded by the canopy, and you will still find this tree at the edge of wooded areas today. The stems that emerge from the base of the tree have proven useful to us for thousands of years, as they are easy to break away; their flexible bendiness is put to all sorts of uses, including baskets, fencing, the frames of coracle boats and more.

Hazel forms natural coppices, and for generations we've also assisted the tree in doing this. In fact, coppicing was the first instance of humans managing woodland for our own purposes, and we're still doing it some 4,000 or so years later. It's not only hazel that can be cultivated in this way. We also coppice sweet chestnut, oak, willow and more. Next time you are walking on the edges of woodland, keep your eyes peeled for the sight of long sticks emerging from a wide flat stump; this is called a "stool". The larger the stool, the older the coppice. A wood that is or has been used for this purpose is called a "copse". If the stool is cut back continuously, the coppice will last indefinitely, an incredible example of sustainability.

The long, whippy stems of hazel are great for basketwork, because the wood is so flexible it can be turned back on itself without breaking, a trait it shares with willow. Hazelnuts, like other nuts, are symbols of fertility; hence testicles are also referred to colloquially as "nuts". And, as you'd expect from a plant that has played such an important part in human lives, the hazel tree has featured in many traditional stories. Sometimes these old tales can be oddly convoluted, as they were spoken, not written.

The ancient Celts believed that hazelnuts could make you wise. In one famous tale, an ordinary salmon unknowingly ate nine hazelnuts that each fell from one of the nine trees of wisdom, with the impressive result that it accidentally ingested all the wisdom of the world. A poet, Finegas, spent seven whole years searching for this fish. At last, he found it, and gave it to his young servant, Ffionn, instructing him to cook it but not eat it, as Finegas planned to do this himself. However, Ffionn, checking to see if the

What does it look like?

Growing to a height of about 12m (39ft) with a similar spread, hazel has a sprawling appearance, with stems that emerge from the base of the tree growing into thickets. The bark is smooth and grey-brown. The alternate heart-shaped leaves are hairy, up to 10cm (4in) long, and a dark green colour that turns to a glowing gold in the autumn months. In late winter to early spring, the pale yellow, dangling catkins containing the male flowers, which appear before the leaves open, are a welcome sight. The female flowers are miniscule, with only a tiny red stigma visible. Hazelnuts start to appear from summertime onward, into the autumn. The shell has a pair of cute little frills, and the edible nuts turn from creamy white to brown when ripe.

fish was cooked, pushed his thumb into the flesh and tasted it. And so all the salmon's wisdom was inadvertently transferred to the boy. Finegas soon noticed that something was different about Ffion; he looked more alert, somehow shinier, glowing. When Ffionn confessed what had happened, Finegan simply gave him the rest of the fish to eat.

After searching for the salmon all that time you'd imagine that Finegas would have been pretty disappointed. But perhaps, being a poet, he was naturally philosophical. Ffion went on to become Ffionn mac Cumhaill, one of the key figures in Irish folklore.

Although often hidden, there's usually more than a grain of truth in stories like this. And the question we have to ask about this one is: Why would we confer all knowledge on a little wild nut? Is it maybe because, as we now know, nuts in general are packed with vitamin E, which can help our brains stay fit and healthy?

Corylus avellana

Wildlife

Early-flowering male catkins are an important source of pollen for bees, and the nuts are gathered by squirrels, dormice and, of course, humans. Moth caterpillars such as the large emerald and the nut tree tussock graze on the foliage, while coppiced hazel gives shelter to ground-nesting birds, including the night jar, nightingale and willow warbler.

Medicinal Uses

Hazelnuts are a source of vitamin E, the antioxidant that helps maintain healthy skin and eyes, and strengthens the immune system. They also contain protein and dietary fibre, which helps keep us "regular". In addition, it has been found that eating hazelnuts lowers the levels of a compound called lipoprotein cholesterol, which is the type of cholesterol that can increase the risk of heart-related issues. However, if you are prone to nut allergies, you need to avoid hazelnuts, along with all nuts.

HAZEL WREATH

A plain hazel wreath is a stylish addition to your garden at any time of year – or you can use it to mark the seasons, weaving in flowers and leaves of your choice.

All you need to make a wreath is a pair of secateurs, some gardening wire or string, and, of course, some whippy young hazel sticks, as long as you can find.

Start by pulling the bendy sticks through your hands to make them even more flexible. Then tie them together to make a circle (this is the trickiest part). After that, it's easy to weave the sticks around your circle – push them, if necessary, to keep the circle as neat as possible. Don't worry if it's not totally perfect, after all you're using a natural material.

Once you're happy, make a hanging loop and add whatever flowers or foliage you like the look of – catkins, budding leaves, blossoms and, perhaps, naturally-dried beech or oak leaves.

HAZELNUT CRACKNELL

You don't hear much about cracknell these days. The name refers to a hard or brittle biscuit or sweet, which I think you will find is a delicious occasional treat.

Makes about 500g (1lb 2oz)

You will need:
250g (9oz/1¼ cups) caster (superfine) sugar
250g (9oz/scant 2 cups) hazelnuts, roughly chopped
(put them in a paper bag and apply a wooden rolling pin)
A good pinch of sea salt

1. Put the sugar into a heavy-bottomed pan and cook over a very low heat until melted and turning a golden colour. Meanwhile, line a baking sheet with baking parchment.
2. Add the hazelnuts, stir well until they are incorporated into the sugar, then take off the heat.
3. Spread the mixture over the prepared baking sheet, sprinkle the sea salt over the sugar and nut mix, and leave to cool.
4. Break with a toffee hammer or a rolling pin, and nibble wisely.

Horse Chestnut

Aesculus hippocastanum

Song: "Rootless Tree" by Damien Rice

The horse chestnut might seem quite common to us now, but in the 18th and 19th centuries it was prized for its rarity and beauty.

The names given to this tree can be quite confusing. Carl Linnaeus, who invented the binomial system of naming plants that gave botanists a universal language, called it *Aesculus* after the Roman term for an edible acorn. However, this isn't an oak tree and neither are the seeds (the conkers) edible – unless you're after a stomach ache.

The "hippo" part of the name means "horse". This might be a reference to the scar left behind on the stem of the leaf. Snap one

off, and if you have keen
eyes (or a magnifying
glass), you'll see that the
scar is shaped much like
a cute little horseshoe,
complete with seven
"nails", which become
clearer as the stem oxidizes.
Finally, *castanum* is a nod to
the perceived similarity with
the sweet chestnut.

*Aesculus
hippocastanum*

Making matters worse, it's
very common indeed for people to
get mixed up between horse chestnuts and sweet
chestnuts (*Castanea sativa*), which are a completely different species.
Just to be clear, sweet chestnut seeds are the deliciously edible nuts
you roast over an open fire at Christmas (see page 168), with Bing
Crosby warbling in the background. Horse chestnuts are the trees
that give us conkers.

Wildlife

The flowers provide a rich and accessible source of pollen and
nectar for various bees and butterflies. The triangle moth
caterpillars eat the leaves, as does the horse chestnut leaf liner
moth. Although the horse chestnut seeds are mildly poisonous
to humans, other mammals, such as deer, relish them.

Medicinal Uses

It's supposed that horses and cattle with respiratory ailments, such
as coughs, were treated with the horse chestnut, and this was
where the name came from. However, this is no longer a common
use, so it's likely either the story is hearsay or the supposed remedy
didn't work. For humans, both Western and traditional Chinese

What does it look like?

This magnificent tree reaches a height of 30m (98ft) or so, with a spread of 20m (around 66ft). The bark of the horse chestnut is a reddish-brown to grey colour. Native to the Balkan peninsula, the tree was first introduced to the UK from Turkey in the 1600s, gradually spreading to the rest of Europe and North America thereafter. This tree has seeded itself all over the place. It is equally at home in mountain forests, in parks, as a specimen tree or in the wild just about anywhere. You'll see the lovely, glossy, brown sticky buds from autumn onward, as it's already thinking about the spring in the middle of winter, followed by distinctive leaves up to 30cm (12in) long. These large divided leaves have

herbalists use horse chestnut extract to help remedy poor circulation, including varicose veins. You can even buy the tablets over the counter at health food stores.

PLAY CONKERS

Richard Mabey, in his astounding book *Flora Brittanica*, relates how the first recorded game of conkers took place on the Isle of Wight in 1848. If you've never played conkers before, here's how you do it. All you need is some nice big conkers, some vinegar, a long nail and some sturdy bootlaces or pieces of string about 25cm (around 10in) long. And a friend to play the game with.

First, select a nice big conker and leave it to soak in vinegar for two minutes to prepare it. Then, make a hole through the middle with the nail and thread your conker onto a sturdy bootlace or piece of thick string, tying a knot at the bottom to stop it from flying off. Now you are ready to play. Take it in turns with your friend to then between five and seven separate leaflets that turn from dark green to orange, yellow and brown in the autumn, creating spatters of colour. In the spring, the flowers start to appear – long structures of many creamy white blossoms up to 30cm (12in) long, standing upright on the branches, just like candelabra. Each flower has a white "lip" that turns to a sexy pinkish-red, filling the air with the most sublime fragrance on warm days. If I made scented candles, I'd definitely try to make one scented with horse chestnut flowers. And if I were a bootmaker, I'd make boots the exact colour of a brilliantly shiny conker (horse chestnut seed), slightly wet, straight from its shell.

try to smack your opponent's conker to smithereens, making sure you hold your conker still on its string while your opponent has their turn. The winner is the person whose conker lasts the longest! There are all sorts of methods of making a winning conker, including baking them in vinegar to harden them. Before conkers came along, kids used hazelnuts in exactly the same way. Except, of course, that hazelnuts are much smaller and more fragile. The new technology of conkers – at least four times the size of a hazelnut, and much harder and way more dangerous – must have been like the equivalent of playing a board game in contrast to a digital console game these days!

HORSE CHESTNUT WASHING LIQUID

The horse chestnut, you might be surprised to learn, is a cousin of the lychee as well as the soapberry. It is known in its native India as *Sapindus*, which gives us the soap nuts that are becoming more and more popular as we strive to find products that are kind to our planet. Like the soapberry, horse chestnuts also contain saponins. It might amaze you to know that they offer a natural resource that works surprisingly well in getting stains out of fabrics, costs nothing, can be used in a washing machine and is totally sustainable. We've been using this wash liquid since we heard of it about 8 months ago from the Watercress Queen (aka Lucie Mann), and it's something of a revelation! Here's how to make it.

You will need:
400g (14oz) conkers (horse chestnut seeds)
3 x 500ml (17fl oz) glass jars

1. Chop up the conkers and dry them, either on a low heat in the oven or in a dehydrator, until they are completely hard. This is to stop them going mouldy. (You can skip this step if you're making the washing liquid straight away.)
2. Put the dried conkers in one of the jars, fill to the top with boiling water and leave for 30 minutes.
3. Sieve, keeping the liquid and pour it into another of the glass jars.
4. Re-soak the conkers for an hour in more boiling water. Sieve again, once more transferring the liquid into a glass jar.
5. Soak the conkers in boiling water again, this time overnight. At this point the slightly acrid scent of the conkers will disappear, and their colour will change from yellow to white.
6. Use the water from the first and second "soaks" to wash the grubbiest clothes, and the third, clearer liquid, for a less soiled wash. Add an eco-friendly (bought) conditioner to the washes, if desired.

The liquid keeps in the fridge for a couple of weeks – label and date it so there's no chance of anyone drinking it! The spent conkers can go straight into the compost or waste food bin.

Juniper

Juniperus communis

**Song: "Boys in the Trees"
by Carly Simon**

The best-known use for juniper berries is, of course, as the ingredient that transforms a base spirit into gin. I have a keen interest in gin (more about which below) and have made recipes for gins that use both common and not-so-common wild plants. The base scent of juniper, although really quite strange, lends itself well to being played with in this context. Juniper is thought to be the only spice that comes from a conifer tree.

Although juniper is so prevalent in many parts of the world, these days most of the berries come from eastern Europe. The very name of the drink, which comes from the French word *genièvre* or the Dutch *genever*, is embedded in the name of the tree. And gin is still incredibly popular these days – in far more salubrious watering holes than in centuries past you can buy just about any flavour or colour that you fancy. It's great fun!

Wildlife

The dense cover provided by mature juniper provides valuable habitat for the goldcrest and firecrest. Other birds, such as the song thrush, ring ouzel and fieldfare eat the fruits. The juniper carpet moth and the chestnut carpet moth feed on juniper, too.

I once worked on a project investigating the plants and foods that had been in constant use since Neolithic times. These included crab apples, oats, hazelnuts, fat hen (white goosefoot), honey, milk and butter (the dairy from aurochs, a cow-like animal now extinct), as well as juniper. It seems that as human beings transitioned from hunter-gatherers to farmers, wherever the land was cleared for planting, both hazel and juniper were left in place as they had great value.

Medicinal Uses

Juniper is an abortifacient, causing spontaneous uterine contractions that can result in a miscarriage. That's why the old, traditional cure for an unwanted pregnancy was for the woman to sit in a hot bath while drinking a bottle of gin. In the 1700s, there was a gin craze in London. The water was filthy, cholera was rife and gin was cheap. The gin houses even had steps at the bar for children to reach for their dose. It's popularity among women was one of the reasons why gin was once called "Mother's Ruin". Grim stuff.

What does it look like?

Juniper can grow to a height of 6m (20ft), which might be surprising to those who know it as a garden shrub. This is an evergreen conifer that can be either bushy and sprawling or tall and imposing.

The common juniper has sharply pointed leaves 12mm (½in) long, carried on shoots that are a little bit blue, a little bit green. The needles are green on the top with a distinctive white band. The juniper "berries" are actually the female cones of the plant, which start out green and ripen to a blackish blue and are about 6cm (2½in) long. Juniper flowers appear in the spring and are tiny. They grow in clusters on separate plants; the male ones are yellow and the female, green. Be aware that both ripe and unripe berries rub along nicely on the same plant. It's the female cones that give us juniper berries, and these take two to three

A smarter use was to take the berries as a contraceptive, as done by Native American tribeswomen. Juniper was also valued as an aid to digestion, as well as a treatment for stomach-related illnesses. Juniper is a diuretic and is helpful as a digestif, to help the body process heavy foods. You'll sometimes see it paired with rich meats for this very reason. The berries were used to eject tapeworms, an issue we thankfully don't see too often these days, but possibly one of the reasons the plant was given special consideration.

Juniper leaves and branches are both aromatic and antiseptic and, because of these qualities, they were burned in the streets of Athens during times of plague. And during a smallpox epidemic in Paris in the 1870s,

Juniperus communis

years to ripen. *Juniperus communis* has, in fact, the widest distribution of any woody plant on the entire planet. Confusingly, the pencil cedar, which was at one time used for making pencils, is actually a juniper and *Juniperus virginiana* is also known as the red cedar.

There are many different varieties of juniper. The low-growing ones are often used in gardens as ground cover. They're tough, drought-resistant and, although they prefer an acidic, limestone soil, this is by no means essential to their survival as long as the ground isn't too wet. Be aware, though, that not all juniper varieties are edible. The berries from the *Juniperus sabina* species are poisonous, so make sure you get the right kind if you intend to grow them for consumption.

they were burned to disinfect the hospitals. Because of the cleansing scent of smoky juniper, the tree is believed to have protective powers.

SMREKA

This refreshing alcohol-free drink from the Balkans is fermented, so it's good for your digestive system as well as tasting lovely and fizzy.
Makes about 1 litre (35fl oz)

You will need:

½ unwaxed lemon, cut into 4, unpeeled

200g (7oz) dried juniper berries

Sugar, to taste (optional)

2 x 1-litre (35fl oz) wide-mouthed bottles

1. Put all the ingredients into the bottle with about 1 litre (35fl oz/ 4¼ cups) water and use a piece of kitchen foil as a loose lid.
2. Leave on a sunny windowsill for between 10 and 15 days. The berries will rise and fall as the mixture ferments, and the hotter the weather the quicker it will ferment.
3. Strain into another, clean bottle, then refrigerate.
4. You can drink your *smreka* as it is or dilute it with fizzy water.

The remaining juniper berries can be used a couple more times to make more *smreka* before the flavour disappears. When you are done with them, just pop them on the compost.

JUNIPER DRAWER SACHETS

The branches and fruits of this tree have insecticidal properties. Collect and crush either or both. Leave them to dry, then place in the centre of a muslin square, gather up the corners and tie with a ribbon. They will keep your wardrobe and clothes drawers fresh-smelling and clear of critters.

Lilac

Syringa vulgaris

Song: "Lilac Wine" by Jeff Buckley

If for no other reason than attracting pollinators, it's worth having lilac in your garden. But there's another reason to love this tree, too – the scent. It's gorgeous. When the blossoms are out and I'm walking my dog, I deliberately pass by a lilac tree that spills over a nearby garden gate for a whiff of that heavenly fragrance. What does lilac smell like? In all honesty, it's a bit old-fashioned. It's sweet, almost cloyingly floral, with the chalky hint of parma violet sweets – hypnotically heavy on a sunny late spring day. This heady scent was a favourite with two American presidents, George Washington (the first President) and Thomas Jefferson (the third). Jefferson planted lilacs at his childhood home, Shadwell, in 1767, and a few years later added lots more at his plantation, Monticello. It's nice to think of such powerful men loving these flowers, and perhaps it would be a good idea if all world leaders spent time gardening.

Lilac is the state flower of New Hampshire, and there are other lilac festivals in Rochester, Spokane, Michigan and in Lombard, Illinois. Lombard's Lilac Time is an annual festival, first held in 1929, in Lilacia Park, featuring more than 700 trees. Like cherry blossoms, lilac blossoms have a gloriously brief moment in the sun, and these festivals celebrate that moment of beauty.

Lilac is yet another tree that, in Greek myth, is transformed from a young nymph into a tree to escape the attentions of a randy god. This time the offender was Pan. The first pan pipes are said to have been made from the hollow stems of the tree.

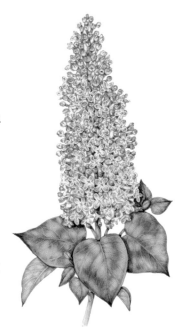

Syringa vulgaris

In Russia, blossoming branches were hung over a baby's crib, to give the gift of wisdom. In Victorian England, lilac signified old loves, and was often worn by widows. This might be why it has ended up with a slightly fusty, fuddy-duddy reputation, which is undeserved. In New England, the trees were planted in order to drive away evil influences. That lovely scent would surely get rid of anything nasty. Also in the USA, it was believed that fresh lilac flowers in the house would drive out ghosts, while in the UK, the opposite was thought to be true – bringing either lilac or elderflower indoors was considered very unlucky, despite these flowers' pleasant aroma. Maybe this particular superstition was invented by servant girls not keen on the extra work of brushing away zillions of tiny petals. Or could it be that introducing flowers or blossoms from trees (as opposed to "normal flowers") into a house was regarded as dangerously pagan?

What does it look like?

Lilac is deciduous, growing to 7m (23ft) tall with a spread of 10m (33ft) in older trees. The bark is a brownish grey with vertical fissures. The leaves are heart-shaped, about 10cm (4in) long. Lilac blossoms profusely for a short but glorious period in late spring to early summer. Native to the Balkan peninsula in southern Europe as well as Iran, lilac is a member of the Oleaceae family, the same as the olive and jasmine.

From its origins the tree has spread widely, mainly because it is grown deliberately in gardens and parks for its colour and especially its scent, but it is occasionally found in the wild. The tree is named for an Arabic word, *lilak*, meaning blue. This description applies to the blossoms, although the long clusters of tiny fragrant flowers also come in white, purple-red, pink and other variations. It's possible that the tree was introduced to Britain sometime during the reign of Henry VIII, as it is mentioned in an inventory taken at Norwich by Oliver Cromwell.

Because lilac is often used as a garden tree, and pruned back, you don't often get to see what it can really look like at its full height and width. The *Syringa* part of the name of the lilac is from the Greek *syrinx*, meaning "pipe" or "tube". This refers to the hollow branches of the plant.

Wildlife

Lilac is pollinated by bees, moths and butterflies, which are attracted to the tree by the fragrant pollen of its flowers. Hummingbirds like its nectar. However, lilac is one of the least desirable sources of food for deer and they tend to avoid it.

Medicinal Uses

Before quinine was extracted from cinchona bark in 1820, lilac was used as to prevent the recurrence of malaria. It has a reputation for being able to lower a fever and to improve digestion simply by eating the flowers (this use is not yet proven). Infused, the flowers can be used as a gargle to freshen the breath. This, I can vouch for!

LILAC VINEGAR

Ridiculously simple, this one. Start by making just half a litre (17fl oz) and see if you like it before making more.

Makes about 70cl (24fl oz)

You'll need:

A good couple of handfuls of lilac

A 75cl (26fl oz) glass jar
A 70cl (24fl oz) glass bottle

1. Put the flowers in the jar, fill it with cold water, and then cover it lightly with muslin (cheesecloth).
2. Leave for a couple of weeks, then strain out the flowers.
3. Decant your vinegar into the bottle and refrigerate. Use as a salad dressing, perhaps with infused bay oil (see page 27).

LILAC POTPOURRI

The small, sweetly scented flowers of lilac make a lovely vintage floral potpourri. Cut whole stems, complete with the flowers, tie them together with string and then pop them, blossoms down, into a paper bag. As lilac blossoms in late spring or early summer, this usually coincides with good weather, so it won't be long before the flowers fall away from the stems, leaving you with a drift of scented petals in the bottom of the bag. Then, leave in a dish in a warm place to bring out that lovely, old-fashioned aroma.

Lime or Linden

Tilia x europaea

Song: Kulikov's "The Linden Tree" by Osipov State Russian Folk Orchestra

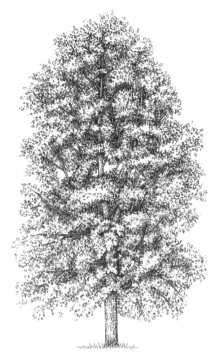

You know how some trees can seem a bit haughty? (I'm certain that it's not just me who feels this about trees.) Linden, however, has a friendly feel about it. Despite its impressive height and beauty, it's always amiable.

The word "lithe" has the same origins as "linden", as does "flexible". They derive from the term for the bast wood, the inner part of the tree that is soft and therefore used in elaborate or difficult carvings.

In my loft I have the smallest doll of an old set of Matroshka dolls, those Russian dolls that all fit inside one another. I've had this little doll since I was a small child. I would have been about eight when, in a fit of generosity I regretted almost instantly, I gave away the other six dolls to my six best friends. I kept the smallest, solid doll for myself, and she makes an appearance every year as part of the Christmas decorations. (If you are reading this and you still have one of those dolls I gave out, I'd love to hear from you). The first-ever Matroshka doll was made in 1890, in Russia. They are made from the wood of the linden tree, which is flexible and easy to work with.

Linden is possibly one of the most useful trees because it is simple to identify and also common. It is easily worked, and great for beginners who want to start carving, as well for as experts who wish to create something particularly ornate. It's even used in making electric guitars. This tree has an absolutely loaded cultural significance, especially in eastern Europe, including the Baltic states, Germany, and also Greece. As well as being considered sacred (and quite frankly, all trees should be considered this way), the lime tree

What does it look like?

There are some 30 different species of lime or linden, and it's also not uncommon for the tree to be confused with the other lime tree – the one that produces green citrus fruits. The tallest of the species is the common lime, which is a hybrid of the small-leaved and the broad-leafed limes, and this tree is the one you're most likely to see.

The common lime grows to a lofty height of 40m (131ft) with a spread of 20m (66ft), often with suckers shooting up from the base of the tree. Linden leaves are lovely – a broad oval shape with tiny, edged teeth. They are a handsome dark green on the top and green and smooth underneath, apart from little tufts of hair. The bark is brownish-grey, showing deep fissures with age. The tree grows wild in woodland areas as well as being the star of the show in parks and the grounds of stately homes. Just like the hazel, the linden is often coppiced. At Westonbirt Arboretum in the UK, there's a linden coppice known to be 2,000 years old.

The flowers of the lime are inconspicuous – just 2cm (¾in) wide, hanging in bracts under the leaves in clusters of between two and five blossoms – but have a scent that's truly sensational. Imagine a fragrance like honey, with a dash of vanilla and a suggestion of jasmine. No surprise that this heady scent has been captured by perfumiers, including in Elizabeth Arden's "Fifth Avenue".

also symbolizes truth and justice. At one time, important judicial matters were discussed beneath the tree. Its high regard is reflected in the fact that the main street in central Berlin is named "Unter den Linden" after the trees that line it. But perhaps my favourite linden story is the Baltic myth of Laima, the goddess of fate, who is named for the tree, and appeared as a cuckoo to give her prognostications. The women of the Baltic States apparently talked to the lime trees as though they were human beings.

Tilia x europaea

Wildlife
No wonder the bees, moths and butterflies love the linden. The lime hawk moth is named after its favourite food, and beekeepers say that linden blossom honey is one of the best in the world.

Medicinal Uses
Linden tea, which is made by infusing both the blossom and the bract (the part found above the leaves but below the flower) is popular in mainland Europe but not so much in the UK or the USA. This needs to change! If you can get your children gathering them and drinking the tea, it can sooth irritability, clear coughs and colds and help your little ones get to sleep. I've found that if you can involve your kids in picking their own remedies (under supervision, of course), then their connection with the tree or plant means that the remedy is way more effective than buying something over the counter. For adults, linden tea is an effective stress-remover. In addition, this same simple tea helps bolster your immune system and reduces cholesterol. It is a tonic for the digestive system,

especially for people who might be on the go a lot of the time. But be aware that linden can have a sedative effect, so avoid drinking it before driving or operating machinery. The flavonoids and glycosides in the little flowers also help bring down the fever that accompanies flu; in this instance, drink the tea hot as you can, have a soothing warm bath and go to bed. My good friend Henry Ashby used to gather thousands of linden flowers and leave them to dehydrate on large cardboard trays, so that he could supply the older members of his community with beneficial tea (see below). The magic wasn't just in the flowers, but also in his caring.

HENRY'S LINDEN TEA

Nothing could be easier. Pick the blossoming lime flowers, as well as the pale green bracts, and dry them in the summer to be used in the winter. Place 2 or 3 teaspoonfuls of dried linden flowers in a mug and add hot water. Leave to steep for 15 minutes or according to taste. The tea can be drunk hot or cold. If you like, you can also infuse the flowers in honey with a little hot water.

LINDEN CARVING

If you can manage to get hold of the interior (bast) wood of a lime tree, then this is the perfect wood to use to have a go at carving, as it is so soft. Watch out for places where there are linden trees, especially in large gardens of stately homes, since these environments are the sorts of places where trees may be cut back fairly regularly or where you might find fallen branches. It's easy enough to whittle away at the outer bark to get to the soft inner wood, but ask permission before taking any timber. A good way to start carving is to take a good look at the wood, follow whatever the shape suggests and see how you go. Make sure you have a clean, sharp knife, and carve away from your body, not toward it.

Magnolia

Magnolia x soulangeana and *Magnolia grandiflora* (ABOVE)

Song: "Magnolia Trees" by The Mayries

Magnolia trees – what show-offs they are! All members of this family are beautiful, with rich flowers and luxuriant foliage. The first time I really noticed one was years ago, when I moved into the first house that was mine rather than one of the rentals I'd endured for several years. It was incredibly exciting, and I was desperate to start re-decorating. A friend advised that I should just paint the whole place magnolia until I knew what I really wanted. I now know that magnolia paint is ubiquitous – the standard blank canvas for rented apartments or for people who can't make up their mind about colours. When I went to the paint store I was really disappointed at the drab, whitish magnolia paint in tins, stacked high on the shelves.

Despite the boring shade of paint named after the tree, there's nothing ordinary about magnolia. For a start, it is very ancient indeed, having been around even before bees came along. The large blossoms were pollinated by primitive wingless beetles, its tough petals adapted to withstand the damage they caused. Magnolia was the first-ever flowering plant. I find it quite mind-blowing that a tree we see commonly in gardens and parks, and that is so very popular, has been with us since the Cretaceous period some 145 to 66 million years ago. To put this into perspective, this tree was around at the

What does it look like?

There are more than two hundred varieties of magnolia, which can be evergreen or deciduous, and small enough to merit the status of a shrub or tall enough to be a tree of 24m (79ft) or more. The saucer magnolia (*Magnolia x soulangeana*) is the most widely found variety in the UK while the southern magnolia (*Magnolia grandiflora*) is favoured in the USA. Whatever variety, they tend to have a sprawling growth habit.

The most definitive feature of this tree is the large, showy, waxy flowers, which generally appear before the leaves, and come in various shades of white, pink, green, yellow and purple. Members of the magnolia clan include the tulip tree (*Liriodendron tulipifera*), and the cucumber tree (*Magnolia acuminata*), whose fruits look a bit like cucumbers, initially being green, but giving way to a bright scarlet. There seems to be a magnolia for all occasions, and although the flowers tend to be quite short lived, their beauty makes up for the brevity of their appearance.

same time as Tyrannosaurus Rex. Next time you see magnolia blossoms over a garden wall, think of how it might look with a dinosaur standing beside it. Or what the plant collectors must have thought when they first encountered the tree.

The tree was named by plant collector Charles Plumier, in honour of Pierre Magnol who, along with Carl Linnaeus, revolutionized the system of naming plants. Magnolia timber is finely-grained, polishes well, and leaves no flavour – it's therefore often made into bowls used for serving food.

Magnolia grandiflora

Wildlife

The early flowers of magnolia provide welcome nectar for insects. These, in turn, attract birds, which love to shelter in the boughs. Magnolia tree pollen is high in protein, and it attracts beetles – as they move from one blossom to another, they pollinate the tree. Squirrels and deer like to nibble on the bark, the latter also eating the leaves, buds and twigs of the magnolia.

Medicinal Uses

Magnolia was once used as a general tonic by the Allegany people of North America; the cones, which contain the seeds, were steeped in spirit to make a tincture. Magnolia is a remedy for rheumatic conditions as well as being a laxative. It is said to help with weight loss, and to counter anxiety and depression. The petals can also be made into a soothing tea that reputedly aids sleep. Practitioners of traditional herbal medicine in Korea, China and Japan use it for a number of ailments. The above remedies may well owe their success to magnolol, a compound that is still being studied, but has been found to be anti-inflammatory and antioxidant, and even to have anti-anxiety and anti-depressant qualities.

MAGNOLIA STILL LIFE

However long it's been since you last drew a picture, it's incredibly relaxing to draw. Magnolia flowers are sensational, so why not pick one (ask permission or pick up one that has fallen from the tree) and bring it home? Then, make yourself a cup of tea, get out some paper and pencils and channel your inner artist to capture the magnolia's beauty. Before you start, study every aspect of the flower very carefully. You may find that you're really rather good at drawing flowers! Either way, it's the enjoyment in trying that counts.

MAGNOLIA SYRUP

A good syrup has many uses, including in cocktails and mocktails, made into ice cream or sorbets, or in other puddings and cakes.

Makes about 2 litres (70fl oz)

You will need:

900g (2lb/4½ cups) sugar

2 x 300ml (10½fl oz) mugs of magnolia petals and buds, roughly chopped

A 2-litre (70fl oz) glass bottle

1. Pop the sugar along with 940ml (32fl oz/4 cups) cold water into a pan. Bring to the boil and simmer until the sugar dissolves. Then remove from the heat straight away.
2. As soon as the water is cool enough for you to put your finger in, add the flowers and buds.
3. Allow to steep for a day, then strain out the flowers.
4. Pour into the glass bottle, seal and store in the fridge.

Maple

Acer pseudoplatanus, Acer campestre
and *Acer saccharum* (ABOVE)

Song: "Maple Glazed Donut" by James Newton Howard

If you have maple trees anywhere near you, please go out in the autumn and gather fallen leaves to bring into the house. There's no need to do anything with them. Just admire them.

Although all maples can be tapped for their (fairly sugary) sap, it's the sugar maple, *Acer saccharum*, also called the bird's eye maple and famed for its maple syrup, which is highlighted here.

The sugar maple is indigenous to the hardwood forests of Canada, from Nova Scotia to Quebec, central and southern Ontario

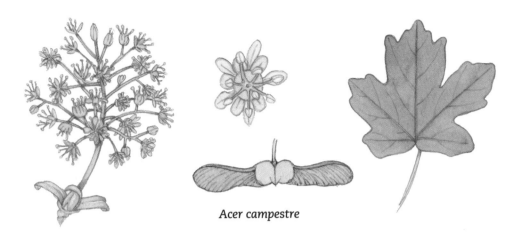

Acer campestre

What does it look like?

This tree family is extensive; it encompasses over a hundred species.
However, all maple species are easy to identify, as all of them have
two features in common. The first is that maple seeds have a
distinctive pair of "wings" that spin as they fall. (This sort of seed is
called a *samara* and the other tree that has them is the ash, although
the ash isn't a maple). The second common feature is the leaf, which
is shaped like an outstretched hand, either with rounded (lobed)
fingers, or pointed ones with more sharply sculpted edges.

Maples can be large, like the sycamore, up to 30m (98ft) in
height, or the Norway maple, a little lower at 25m (82ft). Or there's
the field maple, also called the hedge maple or common maple,
whose leaves in the autumn are so golden they look drenched in
sunshine. Then there's snake bark maple, the Balkan maple, and
the evocatively named full moon maple, native to Japan, with its
delicate feathery leaves and tiny red blossoms. Maples are often
planted in parks and gardens, because they are elegant trees with
a spectacular range of autumn colours, like a living paint pallet.

and further south toward Tennessee and Virginia in the USA. (You'd be forgiven for thinking that the sugar maple is the tree that appears on the Canadian flag, but this isn't the case – it's a mixture of different maple leaves).

When I moved into my current house on a late autumn day five years ago, I inherited a beautiful red maple. I saw it at its finest just days before a sudden storm blew every single leaf from the tree. In the days following, we spent most of our time in the cold and wet, raking in the maple leaves and piling them on the bonfire where they smouldered sulkily for hours. This was far more fun than sorting through boxes of stuff. As we were doing this, a passer-by popped his head over the fence to say hello. He mentioned that our raking and bonfire reminded him of the time he was a lumberjack in Canada. He also said that there was something about maple leaves and bonfires that protected people against the common cold. I do wonder if the very act of ignoring the weather and doing physical work outdoors might be an answer? We tend to stay indoors when it's cold, in overheated houses that are a breeding ground for viruses. Smouldering fires of various sorts of wood have been used for thousands of years in a protective way – hence the word "fumigate". Burning incense is an iteration of this idea.

I also started to think about maple trees and specifically, maple syrup. Why, I wondered, is it produced in Canada but not in other places around the world? The reason that the sugar maple grows where it does is all to do with climate. The seeds need a proper hard freeze to germinate. We're talking regular winter temperatures of -18°C (0°F). Furthermore, the seed germinates only at temperatures of 0–8°C (32–46°F); this is unique among the tree fraternity. As our planet warms, the sugar maple forests are diminishing.

The importance of maple syrup to the people who discovered its qualities – which is likely to have been the Algonquins – can't be underestimated. Travellers' journals from 1609 onward record that the indigenous peoples had a process for taking the liquid from the tree. Maple trees exude "sapcicles", icicle-shaped stalactites of solidified sap that gather at the ends of the broken twigs. This sap is clear, sticky and sweet. It's likely that the sweet stuff oozing from the sapcicles inspired the idea of tapping the tree. Native Americans were, understandably, very fond of maple syrup, so much so that they would relocate to woods where the maple trees were plentiful at the coming of spring when the sap started rising. These "sugar camps" stayed in situ for a month or more. The gatherers would simply make a slash in the tree and collect the sap, as it trickled out into a pot or other vessel. In the 1790s a more sustainable way of tapping trees developed, which is pretty much the same technique used by tree foragers today. The method of boiling down maple syrup to thicken it and bump up the flavour might have been developed by French settlers. One way of eating the syrup was to pour it onto frozen snow and eat it just like that! These days, maple syrup is an important commodity for the places that have maple trees – and if you think it's expensive, bear in mind that it takes about 40 gallons of sap to make just one gallon of syrup.

Wildlife

Sycamore and field maples are attractive to aphids, which in turn are eaten by a variety of moth caterpillars, such as the sycamore moth and the maple prominent moth. The blossoms provide a good source of nectar and pollen for bees. The seeds of maple trees are not only enjoyed by birds, but also by mammals such as squirrels and chipmunks and, on occasion, moose.

Medicinal Uses

Depending on the species, the bark, wood and sap of the maple have various medicinal uses. Native Americans traditionally used the tree to fix a wide range of ailments, from aches and pains to persistent coughs.

HOW TO TAP MAPLE TREES

All the maple family – and a few others, such as birch and beech – can be tapped, but always be careful to plug the hole afterwards. Hammer a small hole into the tree – higher rather than lower but within easy reach – and insert either a grooved stick or a metal spile (spout) into the hole to capture the sap and channel it into a container. Do this when the sap starts to rise in the early spring. The sap can be boiled down to make syrup or used as it is to make beer.

MAPLE SMOKED VEGETABLES

An easy way to use maple leaves was discovered by my partner, Liam. He's a very inventive chef and one day he squirrelled away a few basketfuls of the dried maple leaves we were sweeping up. I wondered what on earth he was up to. He put the leaves in a tray of water in a low oven, with a second tray above it containing slivers of coloured root vegetables, such as heritage carrots in purple, bright yellow and orange, beetroot and parsnips and, later, red, yellow and white swiss chard. The maple leaves suffuse the vegetables with a lovely earthy, smoky flavour. It's really delicious!

MAKE A MAPLE SCRAPBOOK

Collecting leaves is a great, hands-on way to help you identify and appreciate trees, and because maple leaves are some of the most beautiful of all, they are a very good place to start. Paying close attention to the way the maple leaves change through the seasons – as the trees go from buds to full leaf to blossoms and into their glorious autumn blaze of colour – gives us a wonderful opportunity to tune in to the natural cycle of the seasons. You could press the leaves you collect into a scrapbook, noting the dates and places where you find them. There is nothing to stop you widening this activity to include other trees, and maybe blossoms, too.

Medlar

Mespilus germanica

Song: "The Orchard" by Todd Baker

The "*germanica*" part of the botanical name of this interesting tree is misleading because the tree actually originates from southwest Asia. The medlar can be found growing wild occasionally, mainly in southeastern Europe, but the tree is cultivated in many places, too. Excitingly, a new species of medlar was discovered not long ago – in Arkansas in 1990. Called *Mespilus canescens*, it is very rare, with all 25 trees of the new species growing in the same small, protected wood. The medlar is the sort of tree you might spot in walled gardens in the grounds of stately homes, but it is not common. In short, you might see these interesting fruits in a farmers' market, but in a supermarket? Unlikely!

The medlar has possibly the most aptly descriptive, if rude, nicknames for a fruit, ever. It was called "open-arse" by Shakespeare, "autumnal excreta" by D H Lawrence and it translates from the French *cul de chien* as "dog's bottom".

Poor medlar fruit! Insulted, laughed at, scorned and reviled, all because of its appearance. I'm quite fond of trees and fruits that go out of fashion, for whatever reason. I've noticed that the fruit and vegetables we find in "normal" stores are a bit "same old, same old". This means we are in danger of losing diversity and a wider range of choices in favour of mass production, unless, of course, we can afford produce from those lovely famers' markets, or if we have wealthy friends with old houses and gardens where medlar trees are likely to grow. At risk of sounding like someone's granny, it wasn't long ago that the small, hard Cox's Pippin apples, grown for centuries, were designated as being too small for supermarket shelves. They seemed to disappear overnight. And it's pretty safe to say that the medlar isn't exactly a supermodel of the fruit world either, as far as looks are concerned! Even if you've never seen one in real life, you'll know that those unflattering nicknames are accurate descriptions. And be warned – there are aspects of the appearance and attributes of this fruit that might be off-putting. For example, you wouldn't be happy if you bit into a medlar. They need to be bletted (left to go over-ripe) before you can eat them but, once bletted, medlars taste sweet – a little bit like dates.

Put simply, this is a step beyond the more usual ripening process that some fruits need to undergo. To be frank, bletting is a more polite word for "rotting". If this makes you uncomfortable, bear in mind that the fermentation process is also a form of rotting, giving flavour to chocolate, cheese and game meats. For some fruits, bletting brings out a sweetness that wouldn't be apparent otherwise. While the medlar is only really edible after bletting, others just taste sweeter – for example quince, persimmons, sloes and rowan berries. The word was coined relatively recently, in the early 1830s, but I'm

Mespilus germanica

certain that we would have known for a long time that some fruits taste much sweeter when allowed to go slightly over the hill of ripeness.

The issue with medlars is that they're at their best when they look their worst – just refer back to that elegant description, "autumnal excreta" by D H Lawrence. Bletted medlars have the appearance of soggy brown lumps. We aren't used to eating food that looks like this, but if we gave it some thought, we would admire our ancestors, who didn't have supermarkets and were far more experimental with their food.

If you can find a supply of medlars, harvest them in the autumn, when they are hard and dry. Then, layer them in sheets of brown paper, leave in a cold dry place and check them every week or so. When they are ready, they will be brown and smell of ripe apples. Push your finger into them and if they're squidgy, then they're ready to go.

What does it look like?

Medlar trees are deciduous, occasionally having thorny shoots. They reach a height of 6m (20ft) and have a spread of 8m (26ft). The bark of a medlar tree is a mixture of orange, grey and brown. The leaves have an oblong shape and are jagged toward the tips, dark green in colour and quite noticeable, as they reach up to 15cm (6in) in length. Medlar flowers are borne singly, have five white petals and are up to 5cm (2in) wide. After the flowers fall, the fruits start to develop. These are either rounded or pear-shaped. Five long sepals surround the flat-topped inner fruit, which has a central indentation called "the eye".

Wildlife

Medlar fruits provide food for a variety of birds, such as blackbirds, thrushes, and fieldfares. Foxes, rabbits and mice also enjoy the fallen fruits. Medlars are an especially useful food source for wildlife because the fruits tend to stay on the tree into the winter months.

Medicinal Uses

In folk medicine, the medlar was traditionally used to treat diarrhoea, although this usage is no longer popular, perhaps because the fruit isn't seen very often these days. However, research carried out in Turkey has found that medlar bark and leaf extracts contain antioxidants that are helpful in the fight against cancer. Medlar fruits also contain immunity-boosting vitamin C.

MEDLAR KIMCHI

Here's a radical idea. Since medlars want to rot, why not turn them into a healthy and very tasty kimchi?

Makes 2 large jars

You will need:

500g (1lb 2oz) well-bletted medlar fruits

A 4cm (1½in) chunk ginger, shredded

A whole garlic bulb, shredded

10 peppercorns

10 shallots or spring onions (scallions), finely chopped

A dash of Shio Koji (available from health food shops)

2 x 1-litre (35fl oz) glass jars

1. Combine all the ingredients, then divide between the jars and seal.
2. Leave to ferment; the temperature of your kitchen will have an effect on the time the kimchi takes to ferment. Have a taste every couple of days or so, to check its progress. When it's ready it will have a fizzy, slightly acidic tang to it. Once ready, store in the fridge.

Shio Koji is a useful vegan liquid ingredient, made from cooked rice or soya beans inoculated with a fermentation culture. The natural sweetness of the medlars, with the addition of the other ingredients, gives a delicious umami flavour to this kimchi, making it an excellent condiment or side dish with Asian foods. Fermentation is an interesting process, not always predictable, but the benefits of the fermentation process on gut bacteria really can't be underestimated.

MEDLAR PUDDING

Serves 4–6

You will need:

85g (3oz/7 tbsp) demerara (turbinado) sugar
70g (2½oz/6 tbsp) caster sugar
600g (1lb 5oz/2⅔ cups) unsalted butter, softened, plus extra for greasing
2 medium eggs
180g (6¼oz/1⅓ cups) plain (all-purpose) flour
1 tsp baking powder
1 tsp bicarbonate of soda (baking soda)
1 tsp ground cloves
½ tsp salt
200g (7oz) bletted medlar pulp
85g (3oz/⅔ cup) walnuts or hazelnuts, crushed
Double (heavy) cream or ice cream, to serve

1. Preheat the oven to 180°C/350°F/gas mark 4 and grease a 20 x 20cm (8 x 8in) baking pan.
2. Beat together the sugars and the butter, then add the eggs and beat until combined.
3. Stir in the flour, baking powder, bicarbonate of soda, cloves and salt. Mix well, then add the medlar pulp and nuts. Stir very well.
4. Transfer the mixture into the prepared baking pan and bake for 30 minutes until golden brown, turning halfway through.
5. Spoon into dishes and top with cream or ice cream of your choice.

Monkey Puzzle

Araucaria araucana

**Song: "Cactus Tree"
by Joni Mitchell**

Not far from where I live there's an
unused reservoir, often mistaken for a lake. It's
in an unusual spot, as you have to cross a rickety
old metal bridge to get to the woods at the other
side. This bridge is a bit hit and miss, and always
makes me grit my teeth when I walk across its
rusted iron rails, the cold, deep water visible
through the gaps. Once we are safely across, my
dog likes to clamber about in a tumbledown, old
Welsh longhouse right at the edge of the lake,
which is no doubt full of interesting scents for
her, and then we take a longer walk through the
woods. We'd been there lots of times before, but
one rainy summer's day, we came face to face with the trunk of a
tree I'd never noticed before. This particular wood is overgrown and
tangled, difficult to get through in the winter and pretty much
impossible in the summer, as the canopy is so dense that you can't
see the tops of the trees through the leaves. And peering up into the
trunk of this particular tree didn't make me any the wiser. The base
of the tree looked curiously like the foot of an elephant.

On subsequent dog walks I realized that there were two more of
these mysterious tree trunks, and I promised myself I'd come back
in the winter when it might be easier to see what was going on.

Between Christmas and New Year, with nothing much to do, we
went back to the woods. This time, I could see the tops of the trees
from the iron bridge; three very tall, very elegant monkey puzzles,

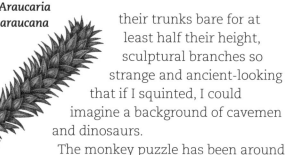

Araucaria araucana

their trunks bare for at least half their height, sculptural branches so strange and ancient-looking that if I squinted, I could imagine a background of cavemen and dinosaurs.

The monkey puzzle has been around for at least 200,000 years – so my imaginings were spot on. It's strange to think that the thick, spiny leaves covering the branches of the tree developed to prevent dinosaurs from snacking on them. The botanical name, *Araucaria araucana*, is named for the Araucanian people who harvested and ate the large seeds of the plant.

If you're taken with the idea of growing a monkey puzzle in your garden, be aware that it could last for a thousand years. And as for that unusual name, which is oddly descriptive? It was coined in the 1850s, at Pencarrow Gardens in Cornwall, UK. The owner, Sir William Molesworth, later became Secretary of State for the former colonies.

What does it look like?

Also called the Chilean Pine, the monkey puzzle tree is native to Chile as well as to western Argentina. It is an unusual-looking evergreen tree which, once seen, is never forgotten. Growing to a height of 30m (98ft) and with a spread of 15m (49ft), the crown of the tree is nicely rounded. It has overlapping leaves that can stay attached to the tree for many years and shoots thickly covered in glossy dark green, oval leaves, which terminate in sharp points. The bark is grey and wrinkly. Male and female flowers grow on separate trees. The male flowers are cylindrical, the females a rounded, ball shape.

Molesworth bought and planted the first-ever monkey puzzle in the UK, at a cost of 20 guineas. The name was accidentally coined by a visiting friend, Charles Austin, who suggested "… it would puzzle a monkey to climb one of those!" The name just stuck. By the way, that 20 guineas would be close to £13,450 (around $19,000) these days.

This tree oozes ancientness (if such a word exists). Although it has the status of a "living fossil" because of its great age, tragically the monkey puzzle is now under threat in its native habitat because of logging, grazing and also fires.

After discovering all this, I started to think about how and why three mature monkey puzzle trees had ended up growing in an unruly, untended wood at the edge of a reservoir in mid-Wales. They certainly didn't get there by accident. Even now, monkey puzzle trees are expensive to buy and not that easy to get hold of. Then, I remembered the old Welsh longhouse and started to ask around. This dwelling originally housed both the family and the cowhouse under the same roof, the humans at one end, the cattle at the other, with a passage in between. The house and its grounds had been purchased outright by the water authority when the reservoirs were constructed in the late 18th and early 19th centuries. It's possible that the tangled woods the trees stood in had once been the pastures and gardens belonging to the house, though I doubt I'll ever know for sure. Foraging is never just about gathering plants.

Wildlife
Jays and squirrels feast on the tasty nuts of the monkey puzzle, dispersing the nuts as a result. In its native South America, the tree provides a home for the slender-billed parakeet, and a number of endangered insects, including the native bumblebee, the moscardon.

Medicinal Uses
Resin from the monkey puzzle is traditionally used in the treatment of ulcers and other wounds.

EATING MONKEY PUZZLE SEEDS

The seeds of the monkey puzzle tree are well worth searching for. Make a note of wherever you see a tree and visit it any time between early autumn and mid-winter to see what you can find on the ground. The large cones are green-gold in colour and grow from the tips of the branches. The cones take up to three years to mature after which they open, releasing the nuts, which are a red-gold colour and up to 4cm (1½in) long, with a dark brown tip. I haven't seen anything that looks remotely like them.

The nuts have a soft shell, which is easily sliced open with a sharp knife. I'm not going to offer any fancy recipes since the nuts taste so good just as they are, sliced end to end leaving the shell on, and popped into a hot oven for ten minutes or so. They taste like a cross between pine nuts and sweet chestnuts, with a sweet flavour and a tender, mealy consistency. I think they're just about my favourite nut.

GROW YOUR OWN MONKEY PUZZLE TREES

Sadly, the monkey puzzle, the "living fossil" that is the Chilean national tree, is now endangered. Logging practices caused a long decline in the tree's security, and although those practices were banned in 1990, further damage was caused to the monkey puzzle forests in the years of 2001–02 by devastating fires. Further ancient trees, known to be at least 1,300 years old, were also destroyed and other threats, include grazing by livestock and human harvesting of the seeds have meant that fewer new trees are growing.

But maybe we can help. How about raising monkey puzzle trees from seed to help fight back their decline?

Here's how to germinate, look after and eventually site your own monkey puzzle trees.

- **Seeds:** If you can't find the seeds yourself, you can buy them all year round from larger garden centres as well as online sources.

Prices vary but still amount to pennies or cents rather than pounds or dollars for a good handful of ten or so seeds.

- **Planting:** Monkey puzzle trees are not that fussy. Sow in trays or pots of a 50/50 mix of standard compost (preferably not peat, which is not a sustainable) and sharp sand. The mix needs to be damp, not wet and certainly not waterlogged.

    You'll see that the seed has a sharp end. Push this sharp end down into the compost to half its length and then either seal the planted seeds in a polythene bag, or place in a propagator. Put the planted seeds in a place with an even temperature of 20–25°C (68–77°F).

- **Germinating:** The seeds should germinate within a few days – look, but don't disturb them. As the seedlings start to show, open the container and see what's going on. You may notice that some of the seeds are pushing themselves free of the compost. This is because the roots are developing!

- **Transplanting:** Transplant any rooted seeds into 1-litre (35fl oz) pots of a good-quality seedling compost and move them to a cooler position of between 18–21°C (64–70°F). An average indoor temperature is fine. Water the seedlings sparingly and keep them in a light place.

    In early summer, the baby monkey puzzle seeds can be planted out in a sunny position. You may prefer to put them in bigger pots while you decide the best place to site them.

- **Siting:** Bear in mind that these trees will grow to a great height and a great age. In contemplating their permanent home, consider what changes the trees would make in the landscape. Would they be too close to houses or other buildings? Would they make shade where you want sun? What other plants would be affected by them? The trees you are planting are for the future and will be around long after you've fizzled out. But what a sensational legacy to leave behind.

Mulberry

Morus rubra, Morus nigra (ABOVE)*, Morus alba* and
Broussonetia papyrifera

Song: "The Hole in the Hedge" by Martin Hayes

Somewhere in the depths of your memory you might have a vague
recollection of a connection between mulberries and silkworms.
You may recall that silkworms are among the creatures that eat just
one thing, and one thing only – specifically, the leaves of the white
mulberry. Without the white mulberry, there would be no silkworms
and no silk either. Silk is made from the gossamer thread of the
silkworm's cocoon; this continuous thread is some 100m (109yds)
long. It works like this: the worms constantly eat the leaves of the

white mulberry for six weeks or so then, when they are about 8cm (3¼in) long, they turn into caterpillars and start to spin their cocoon in a figure-of-eight pattern. This takes three to eight days. The cocoon itself is the size of a small egg, 8–10cm (3¼–4in) or so long. Once the cocoon is made the worm encloses itself, ready for the process of eventually transforming into a beautiful cream-coloured silkworm moth. However, this transformation doesn't take place in a silk factory. The cocoon is gently taken apart, the "glue" that holds it together removed, and the cleaned threads wound onto a reel. Knowing this, we might wonder how silk scarves can be purchased so cheaply!

In the early 17th century, King James I was so keen to establish a silk industry in Britain that in just one year, from 1609 to 1610, he planted 10,000 mulberry trees in what is now the centre of London. However, he missed one crucial aspect of the operation – that the silkworm eats only white mulberry leaves. Unfortunately, the 10,000 trees were black mulberries. I can't help but feel sorry for this long-dead king. And if you've ever heard the rhyme "Here we go round the mulberry bush", you might have wondered where it came from. Rumour has it that the song came about in a women's prison in Wakefield, Yorkshire, where the inmates exercised by walking round and round the bushy tree in question.

Mulberry fruits are delicious and incredibly juicy; they bruise easily though, which might be why they don't often appear in markets, lending themselves much better to the safe hands of foragers, who care more for flavour than appearance. Mulberries are a tease, being both sweet and tart. Like raspberries, mulberries keep ripening among the leaves for a decent period of time – up to a month or more – so you can keep gathering them.

Wildlife

Birds, including cardinals, woodpeckers and pigeons, love to eat mulberry fruits, as do foxes, squirrels, raccoons, mice and other animals. Deer nibble on the twigs and leaves. Insects, including spiders and ladybirds, find shelter in the leaves of the tree, whose foliage also provides food for red admiral butterflies.

Medicinal Uses

In Chinese herbal medicine, the powdered leaves of the white mulberry are used to control high cholesterol levels and diabetes. Other claims for mulberry leaf remedies suggest that they help the heart stay healthy and reduce various sorts of inflammation; however, trials are ongoing.

Mulberry fruits contain vitamin C as well as lots of the dietary fibre that we know is good for our digestive system. They are also a good source of iron, calcium and potassium.

Morus nigra

What does it look like?

Here's where you get four trees for the price of one! Each of these mulberries is named for the colour of their juicy fruits. You might be surprised to discover that the mulberry belongs to the same family as the fig.

Indigenous to the USA, the red or American mulberry (*Morus rubra*) is deciduous, grows to a height of 10–15m (33–49ft), and has a slim trunk about 50cm (20in) in diameter. The leaves grow alternately, and they are 7–18cm (3–7in) long and 8–12cm (3–5in) wide, roughly heart-shaped with fine teeth along their edges. These leaves, unlike those of other mulberries, are rough to the touch on the top – almost like sandpaper – and a dull brown colour. The undersides are covered with soft downy hairs. The flowers are small, red or green in colour, and appear at the same time as the leaves. A mulberry tree can live to be 125 years old.

The black mulberry (*Morus rubra*) is the one that you're most likely to see in Great Britain. Also, deciduous, it is in many ways very similar to the red mulberry apart from being a little shorter at 10m (33ft) high. It has the same spread as its American cousin, and is rough and hairy on top, and a deep green colour.

The white Mulberry (*Morus alba*) is native to Asia, but it has travelled so successfully to various parts of the globe that in some places is it regarded as an invasive species, especially in the USA and Brazil.

The species name for this tree is *morus*, for the Greek God of the same name, whose task it was to drive mortal humans toward their fate. The equivalent Roman god was Fatuus, which means fate. *Moros* means "doom" and is the root of the word "morose". But this tree and its fruits are definitely not in the least bit sad or gloomy.

What about the fourth mulberry tree I promised you? The paper mulberry (*Broussonetia papyrifera*) gives us a very fine bark cloth, or "tapa", which is made into a very fine paper that is used by artists and printers.

Mulberry fruits look rather like blackberries that have grown too big for their boots. Beware, though, if you're aiming to cook with them – they stain (your hands, your clothes and anything else you care to mention) more conclusively than any other fruit I know, except maybe for elderberries.

MULBERRY WATER KEFIR

Water kefir is a probiotic, fermented drink full of micronutrients, enzymes and bacteria that are beneficial to gut health. The grains are pretty easy to find online as sachets. Make sure that all your equipment is squeaky clean between batches.

Makes 2 bottles

You will need:

750ml (26fl oz/3¼ cups) filtered
 water
70g (2½oz/⅓ cup) sugar
1 sachet water kefir grains
3 tbsp organic dried fruit of your
 choice, as a starter

½ organic lemon
A large handful of mulberries
A 1-litre (35fl oz) clip-top jar
2 x 500ml (17fl oz) glass bottles
 with screw-tops

1. Heat the water in a pan and pour in the sugar. Allow to dissolve.
2. When the water is almost cool, add the grains, dried fruits, lemon and mulberries to the jar. Pour in the sugar water, making sure there is about 6cm (2½in) of space left at the top of the jar for fermentation to take place. Put the lid on.
3. Place the jar somewhere safe and keep at room temperature. Fermentation should take between one and three days – you will see bubbles coming to the surface.
4. Strain out all the solids, including the grains, and pour into smaller screw-top bottles, leaving 3cm (1¼in) at the top of the bottle. Leave for a couple of days until you can see the contents of the bottle fizzing.
5. Use the grains again to make another batch in the same way. You can also try making water kefir with other fruits and blossoms, including elderflower and elderberries, cherries, plums and many more. Enjoy experimenting!

MULBERRY NATURAL DYE

A couple of years ago my friend Rachel and I spent a few mornings playing around with wild plants to see what colours they would make as dyes. The colours of the plants and their fruits don't always tally with the final result; the cloth and dye fixative (mordant) used also make a difference. We tried various types of paper, and the results were surprising – for example, bright red begonia petals showed red on cartridge paper and grey on printer paper.

Mulberry stains are very difficult to remove from your hands and clothes, so it makes sense to try using your excess mulberries as a natural dye. My own experiments with mulberry resulted in either a soft, pale grey shade or a darker, almost blue-grey colour.

You will need for Stage 1:
½ mug of salt
fabric – use natural fibres, a couple of different types
    such as cotton or silk, if possible

1. Put the salt in a large pan along with 8 mugs of water.
2. Bring to the boil, add the fabric and simmer for an hour.
3. Rinse away the salt, wring out the fabric and clean the pan.

You will need for Stage 2:
3 mugs mulberries

1. Put the mulberries and 8 mugs of water into the same large pan.
2. Smash up the berries with a potato masher and bring to the boil.
3. Put the lid on the pan and simmer for 20 minutes.
4. Let cool a little then strain away the berries.
5. Add the fabric and leave to soak for 24 hours.
6. Take the fabric out the water and rinse until the water runs clear.
7. Hang your fabric to dry and compare the colours. Welcome to your new hobby!

Oak

Quercus robur (ABOVE) and *Quercus alba*

Song: "A Forest" by The Cure

Trees often have alternative names (rowan is "quicken", for example, guelder rose is "crampbark" and elder is "pipe tree"), but oak has fewer of these folk names. And this might be because we believe that the oak, of all trees, is the very personification of a tree. Let me explain. The Indo-European word for oak – *deru* – is also the root of our word "tree" so, alternative names are unnecessary.

There are, however, lots of pet names for individual oaks, as well as oak-themed places in the landscape that tell us a story. Gospel Oak, for example, is a common place name in the UK; and the famous Emancipation Oak in Hampton, Virginia, is where, in 1863, the black community gathered to hear Abraham Lincoln's Proclamation of Emancipation. The tree is still there, telling a story of living history in the grounds of what is now Hampton University.

The oak is the King of the Forest for many of us. But why? Is it because oak trees are so incredibly beautiful? Or because they're long-lived and (unlike the yew, which somehow reeks of the dark mysteries of life and death), the oak has a benevolent, reliable, kindly sort of vibe? Or is it simply because it's one of the easiest trees to identify, and so we're on safe ground and can name it because of its familiarity?

There are several different species of oaks. The most common, anywhere, is the English oak, *Quercus robur*, also known as the pedunculate oak. A peduncle is simply a stalk. Where the English oak is concerned, that peduncle is none other than the short stalk of the leaf, generally hidden by two tiny mini leaves at its base. Also, you should know that the name English oak is a bit of a misnomer, as it grows far and wide.

As far as edibility goes, by many accounts the white oak (*Quercus alba*) is best. If you're in the USA, you're in luck. If you're elsewhere, then the pedunculate oak, which predominates just about everywhere else, also has its edible uses, as long as you remember to soak away its tart, tannic flavours.

The white oak is named for the colour of its timber, not, as some might think, because of its bark. Euell Gibbons, in his splendid book *Stalking the Wild Asparagus*, describes the tastiness of the acorns of this particular species and compares them to sweet chestnuts, advising that we blanch them and coat them in successive layers of sugar, like marrons glacés (which are actually glazed sweet chestnuts, see page 168).

As you're probably aware, acorns have a long history as food for humans; they're calorie rich and, of course, abundant. However, the use of acorns as a food has largely fallen by the wayside in recent

What does it look like?

Oak can grow to a height of 35m (115ft), with a spread of up to 30m (98ft). Its bark is grey, with vertical fissures that grow deeper with age. Long, yellow hanging catkins appear in late spring, and green acorns form on mature trees (over 50 years old) in cupules in late summer, turning brown before they fall to the canopy below. Acorns of the white oak appear singly and are the shape of a small egg with a shallow "cap". Acorns of the pedunculate or English oak (*Quercus robur*) usually appear on notably longer stalks with 2–4 acorns per stalk. Oak leaves are longer than they are wide and grow up to 10cm (4in) long, with short stalks and five or six deep, rounded lobes. The leaves start to appear in spring, turn a yellow-brown in autumn and often hang on well into the winter. Varieties of *quercus* can be found in most countries.

times. For one, they're quite time-consuming to process and, having personally made acorn bread from acorn flour (from English oaks), I reckon our palates have changed too much to find it very palatable. That said, I'd certainly advise that you give cooking with acorns a go (see recipes on page 127). The reason? So that you can get a flavour, literally, of how humans once had to live. After all, it's not so very long ago in evolutionary terms that we hunted and gathered to survive; if we caught or found something nutritious that also tasted good, then that would have been a real bonus. If nothing else, baking acorn bread will make you realize how incredibly lucky you are to have supermarkets, farmers' markets, Deliveroo and so on. And who knows – you might even like it.

I have to admit to you right now that I'm a bit of a stationery nut as well as a tree enthusiast. So finding out how to make oak gall ink, which has been used for at least 2,000 years, was doubly thrilling, and I hope it will be for you, too (see recipe on page 128).

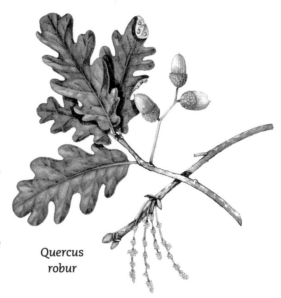

Quercus robur

There are lots of different types of gall, on all sorts of plants – and not just on trees, either. The one we're looking at here is caused by a species of wasp (*Andricus kollari*) that lays her eggs safely inside the bud of a dormant oak leaf. The gall develops so that the larvae of the wasp remain protected – in effect, the young wasp camps out on the tree until it's time to go. Sometimes you'll see the discarded galls in among the leaf litter on the ground; sometimes they stay attached to the tree. Imagine a wooden marble with a tiny little hole in one side.

Also, there's a new oak gall on the block. The oak knopper gall (created by the wasp species *Andricus quercuscalicis*) is a lumpy, bumpy, chunky thing, relatively new in Britain and the USA, having arrived in the 1950s from Scandinavia. The knopper gall starts out bright green and is ripe (and ready to use as ink) when brown and woody. The bad news for the oak tree is that the *Andricus quercuscalicis* gall can sap its nutrients and energy; the other kind doesn't do any harm at all. The good news for you is that both types of galls contain tannic acid, which makes them equally good for making ink.

But first, some history. The first written mention of oak gall ink comes from Pliny the Elder, who was a naturalist, author and philosopher and is credited with devising the first encyclopaedia.

He died around AD 79, a decent indication that the ink was in use for some time before that date.

Oak gall ink is not only very black in colour, it's also easy to make and indelible. Important documents written in oak gall ink include the Codex Sinaiticus (the earliest surviving Bible, written in the 4th century AD), the Magna Carta (1215) and the American Declaration of Independence (1776). Even today, important official documents (birth and death certificates, for example) are written using inks containing ingredients used in making the original oak gall ink! This ink is indelible, incorruptible, made with organic ingredients that – if you pick up pieces of scrap iron – are virtually free. I find this incredibly thrilling!

Knopper gall and oak apple gall

Wildlife

An oak forest supports a variety of wildlife. Birds, insects, and mammals all rely on it for shelter and food – for example, the caterpillars of the purple hairstreak butterfly eat the flowers, leaves and buds of the tree. The rotting leaf litter at the base of the tree breaks down quickly as the leaves are soft, meaning that not only beetles, such as the stag beetle, but various types of fungi – for example "chicken of the woods" – can thrive. Holes in the bark shelter birds and bats, which eat the insects that shelter in the canopy of the tree.

Medicinal Uses

In the Bach Remedy system, oak is used to "support brave and strong people who never give up the fight". The tannins in oak are very astringent (acidic or bitter), so while oak can be used to treat diarrhoea and dysentery, internal use needs to be limited otherwise nutrients can't be absorbed from the diet. Oak remedies can be taken orally as droplets or in capsule form.

COOKING WITH ACORNS

The following recipe comes in two parts – first, we need to make the acorn flour (or "meal"), and then we make pancakes. Or you can use the flour to make bread, if you'd like to. If you enjoy faffy, time-consuming but interesting culinary experiments, then this will be very much to your satisfaction!

ACORN FLOUR

Find 20 fallen acorns (this way you know they're ripe). Any variety is fine. Pop the acorns into a very low oven for an hour or so to dry out. Let them cool, then grind up with a stick blender (add a little water) as finely as you possibly can. Next, you need to pour water through the flour to get rid of the tannins. Using a muslin (cheesecloth) bag that fits nicely over a bowl, pour cold water through the flour up to six times a day for a week. (I told you it was faffy!) If you're using white oak acorns, you will still need to tame those tannins, but it won't take so long. Just keep tasting. Let dry thoroughly. That's your flour!

ACORN PANCAKES

Now that you have the acorn flour, try making pancakes, which are easier to make and, in my opinion, much tastier than acorn bread. I had a go at acorn pancakes for the first time when I was 16. They weren't great, but I was making it up as I went along. Now, I know lots more about tannins and how to tame them.

Makes approximately 10 small or 15 larger pancakes

You will need:

125g (4½oz) acorn flour

125g (4½oz/1 cup minus 1 tbsp) plain (all-purpose)flour

2 tsp baking powder

2 medium eggs

Pinch of salt

500ml (17fl oz/2 cups) milk

Butter or oil, for frying

1. Mix all the ingredients together thoroughly – if you can, leave the mixture for a couple of hours as it will be much smoother.

2. Melt a little butter in a frying pan and coat the base of the pan with the pancake batter. Fry until set and golden underneath, then flip over and cook the other side. Remove from the pan.

3. Repeat until all the batter is used up. Your acorn pancakes will have a nice nutty flavour.

MAKING OAK GALL INK

The toughest part of this whole shebang is finding the oak galls – and that's not tough at all. Just look upward from underneath the tree at any time from midsummer to midwinter. If there's a little hole, then the wasp has left. You can pick the galls from the tree, or you might find them on the ground. The oak knopper gall is even easier to find and, as I mentioned, also works really well for making ink.

You will need:

Half a 300ml (10½fl oz) jar of smallish bits of rusty iron, such as old nails (failing that a ball of steel wool)

Vinegar or lemon juice, to cover the iron bits

A dozen or so oak galls

6 or so drops of liquid gum arabic (easy to find in art shops or online), to aid ink flow (optional)

A clear 300ml (10½fl oz) jar with lid, plus label

1. First, cover your collection of rusty stuff in the jar with the vinegar or lemon juice. Place a piece of cardboard over the top and leave for a couple of weeks. Don't be tempted to close this jar with a lid – the mixture needs to "breathe".

2. Take your galls and smash them up in a controlled way – a pestle and mortar is fine as long as you're fairly gentle, so you don't end up with gall shrapnel littering the kitchen. Otherwise, put the galls in a sturdy plastic bag and apply brute force with a brick (outdoors, please). You're aiming to make a fine powder.

3. Pop the gall powder in an old pan and cover with water. Bring to the boil and then simmer, covered, adding a little water now and again, so that the pan doesn't run dry. This process will take an hour or so.

4. Leave to cool, then strain the bits out with a tea strainer lined with a little piece of muslin (cheesecloth). The finer the grounds of gall, the finer your ink will be.

5. Pour the liquid into the clear jar – you'll be using roughly the same volume of the vinegar mix, and a clear jar means you can see how much you'll need. Leave until cold.

6. Strain the liquid from the iron and vinegar mix into a jug or jar, keeping the rusty stuff for further batches of ink. Then, pour the vinegar solution into the gall mixture; you should see an immediate reaction as the ingredients say "hello!" to one another. Add a few drops of gum arabic, if using and give it all a good stir. Put the lid on the jar and label it.

Have a play around with writing implements to use with your ink – cheap wooden skewers are good, as are bamboo pens. Just avoid using your favourite old-style fountain pens, as your homemade ink will cause them to seize up.

Experiment with different surfaces. I've found that printer paper works well, as does any tree bark that peels away easily without harming the tree.

Olive

Olea europaea

Song: "Wendell Gee" by REM

Look again at the jars of olives or bottles of the oil that you see in a supermarket. It's easy to take such things for granted, but the olive tree really deserves to be highlighted for many reasons. Don't worry if you don't like olives, by the way – they're still a part of your life whether you like it or not. I didn't like them at all until my early thirties. As a kid, I'd seen them sitting next to cheese and crackers at Christmas but wasn't allowed to eat them. So, when I was 12, I bought a jar of the stuffed ones, with red bits sticking out of the ends, not only with the idea that they'd make a more interesting playtime snack than crisps and bananas, but also hoping to impress everyone with my sophistication. Tragically, everyone, including me, spat them out immediately and my ambitions for street cred, already pretty low, bit the dust quite definitively. Ah well.

I didn't quite give up on olives after that, but every single one I tried was horrible. However, some Greek friends, Sadahzinia and Michaelis, came to visit and brought with them olives grown and harvested by their family. They showed us pictures of the olive groves, with sheets spread under the trees on which to gather the fruits, which they shook down. Most of these olives were destined to be sent to the local co-operative where they would be treated and packaged. However, along with the pressed oil, they kept some of them for family and friends, including me. And, good heavens, they were delicious! The oil, too, tasted fragrantly of the olives – creamy and delicate. It was a hot summer and we played backgammon, ate the olives and sipped wine as though the Mediterranean climate had transferred miraculously to mid Wales. Our guests didn't know what variety of olives they were; they had just "always been there". Given that there are olive groves in Mediterranean areas that have been bearing fruit for 2,000 to 3,000 years, I wonder if the olives we were eating were of that provenance? I'll never know, so let's say "yes".

Olive trees originated in the Mediterranean basin, a vast area that covers three continents: Europe, Asia and Africa, in landmasses that wrap themselves around the Mediterranean Sea. This is where human beings began the deliberate cultivation of the tree some 7,000 years ago. Fossil evidence tells us that the olive tree has been growing for between 20 and 40 million years. As well as in their original home, olive trees are cultivated in Morocco, Syria, Portugal and even in parts of China and India. The word "oil", something we all take for granted, is itself derived from the Greek word for olive oil, *elaion*, which became the Latin *oleum* and the Old French word *oile*. The oil was also traditionally used in lamps – the brightness giving the olive tree a connection with light and hope.

What does it look like?

It might be a surprise to learn that the olive tree, which is an evergreen, can grow to a height of 15m (49ft). It's usually cut back though, to make it easier to gather the olives, with the result that it's generally seen as a shrubby-looking tree with low-hanging branches. It has narrow leaves up to 8cm (3¼in) long, which are grey-green on the top and white-grey on the underside. Clusters of tiny white flowers in the summer are followed by the olives, stone fruits or "drupes" (like a cherry or a peach), which ripen from green to black.

The olive will grow fairly happily in some of the colder countries of the world, provided it is grown in a pot and protected from harsh weather. It's when you see the endless rows of short, gnarly, grey-green olive trees, though, that you see them at their best, complete with dusty, scrubby ground, the scent of wild thyme and heat haze in the distance. And think of the religious and cultural significance of the olive! The branch is a powerful symbol of peace – an invitation to share bounty and to transform an enemy into a friend. According to Greek myth, the goddess Athena was given the privilege of having the city of Athens named after her when she gave the city the gift of an olive. There's still an old folk remedy that lingers: to cure a headache, write the name of Athena on an olive stone and hold it to your head. However, I can't tell you whether or not this works. If you eat little or no meat, including nutritious olive oil in your diet will help keep you fit and healthy. The tree was so revered in the ancient world that harming an olive tree was a punishable offence. Followers of Islam believe that each of the names of Allah are written on the leaves.

As well as being tough, olive wood has really beautiful patterning. It is used for chopping boards, spoons, pestles and mortars and, if you're wealthy, larger items of furniture.

Wildlife

Birds and various mammals love olives and help them grow by eating the fruits and scattering the pits. Olive plantations in Mediterranean areas such as Greece, which are often hundreds of years old, make up an ecosystem that can support some 200 species of wild plants, 90 or so vertebrates and 160 invertebrates per hectare. These include owls, hoopoes, lizards and many insects.

Medicinal Uses

High in monounsaturated fatty acids, which lower the risk of heart disease, the olive is a key ingredient in the "Mediterranean diet", said to be the world's healthiest regime. As an infusion, the leaves help to lower high blood pressure, act as a laxative and also soften earwax – if you've ever seen tiny bottles of olive oil in pharmacies, that's that they are for. If you have a build-up of wax in your ear, get a friend to drip just two or three drops of warmed olive oil into your ear, and massage the skin the front of your ear canal to help the oil get to where it needs to go. Olive oil makes a great carrier for massage oils, too.

OLIVE TAPENADE

This lovely salty spread is named after one of its ingredients – capers, or *tapenas* in Provençal. If you like, replace the anchovies with chopped sundried tomatoes.

Makes about 300g (10½oz)

Olea europaea

You will need:

1 x 290g (10¼oz) jar olives (not the stuffed ones) in oil, drained, plus 50ml (1¾fl oz/ 3½ tbsp) oil from the jar

1 tbsp capers

2 anchovy fillets or equivalent sundried tomatoes

1 tsp balsamic vinegar

Black pepper

Sprig of thyme or basil, to serve

1. Blitz all the ingredients, except the herbs, with a stick blender.
2. Add a twist of black pepper and the herbs to serve. I like to eat this with friends, just as it is, on warm crusty bread.

OLIVE-PIT WORRY BEADS

If you eat a lot of olives, you'll also have a lot of pits (unless you eat the pitless, stuffed variety that I fell foul of). If so, why not use them to make olive-pit worry beads, also known in Greek as *komboloi*? The Greeks use these beads to keep their fingers busy and relieve tension, but most of all they are just fun to play with!

Traditional worry beads have an odd number of beads, as well as one bead that's larger than the others, known as the "shield" bead. If you eat mixed olives, you're likely to have differently sized pits and you should be able to find a larger one.

The length of a loop of worry beads is approximately two handwidths of the person you're making them for, so you'll need beading wire the length of 4 hand-widths, plus extra to accommodate the larger shield bead. You could also add a tassle.

Make sure the olive pits are clean and dry, then carefully drill a hole in each one using a 1mm or 1.4mm jewellers' drill bit depending on the size of the pits. Thread the beading wire through each pit, making sure there's enough space for the beads to move along the thread. Once you've threaded the required number of beads, thread both ends through the shield bead, tie into a knot and attach the tassle, if using.

Peach

Prunus persica

Song: "Family Tree" by Kings of Leon

Some years ago, a friend of a friend (let's call him James) had been given the job of caretaker at Croome Court, a colossal stately home in the UK, just for the winter. He was living all alone in this pile of a place with 15 bedrooms, not including the servants' quarters, which had been inhabited by the same family from the 16th century until 1948. The grounds were the first-ever project by Capability Brown, and many of the rooms were designed by Robert Adam. Initially, James was delighted and slept in his sleeping bag in a different bedroom every night, a bit like Goldilocks, except without any bears to keep him company ... just him ... and the ghosts. After a few nights of freezing cold silence, interrupted only by strange clicks, rattles and the sound of something being dragged along the wooden floors of the former servants' quarters, he was turning into a wreck. And so a small party of us were invited to stay.

The first thing we did was to get James out of the main house and into a slightly crumbling but cozy gardener's cottage in the grounds. We kept the cottage warm by burning dried-out cow dung, which works really well, costs nothing and isn't as disgusting as it sounds. One day we decided to explore the place properly. The grounds were extensive, and included a curious construction called a "hot wall" in the gardens. In the early 1800s, this was the very latest technological innovation in gardens. This one was the largest in the UK, 100m (109yds) long and 3m (10ft) high. Designed to trap the heat from the sun, it was supplemented by five underground furnaces running along the north wall. This, as well as the 80 or so gardeners who kept things ticking during its heyday, must have cost an absolute fortune. This hot wall, I found, had been built with the sole purpose of growing ... guess what? Peaches.

Peach trees originate in north-west China, and it's China that still supplies most of the world with these sweetly delicious fruits. In some parts of Europe and the USA, the peach tree has naturalized; after the Spanish conquistador Hernando de Soto landed near what is now Tampa Bay in Florida, carrying with him peach fruits, they grew so rapidly that when the European settlers arrived, they assumed the tree was indigenous to the country. The *persica* part of the name tells us that it was once widely grown in Persia (modern Iran), from

Prunus persica

What does it look like?

A peach tree reaches 8m (26ft) in height, with a 10m (33ft) spread. A deciduous tree with smooth shoots, its leaves alternate and are lance-shaped and dark glossy green, tapering to a point. Its blossoms have short stalks with either pink or white flowers that appear before the leaves begin to show (just like the blackthorn). The downy, fuzzy skin and juicy pink flesh hide an unusual grooved and pitted stone, with a creamy white seed inside. A nectarine tree looks very similar, except the fruits are smooth rather than fuzzy.

which country Alexander the Great brought them to Europe. Spanish explorers took them to South America, and from there the tree wended its way to Great Britain in the 17th century where, as you might imagine, their exotically delicious, juicy taste meant that they were very highly prized. And at this point, we are back at that stately home and the hot wall. The peaches that we take for granted today were once an important status symbol and growing them in such a manner – defying all the odds and vagaries of the English climate – must have been the equivalent of having a brand-new Ferrari in the drive, a symbol of one-upmanship that would surely annoy your neighbours for miles around.

And what about the peach itself? In China, the shape of the peach stone, with its complex winding folds, is a symbol of wisdom, immortality and good luck. Peach wood brushes used in Chinese calligraphy were believed to be the best. A stylized version of a peach stone, called a *shou*, is something that you are likely to have seen many times without realizing its significance. It's often hidden in plain view as a motif in Chinese restaurants. In the West, we use the word "peachy" to describe something that is particularly satisfying or fine. I'd like to offer up a further idea, inspired by the ripe, "pinchability" factor of the peach, whose fruit, whatever language you speak, really does look like a pert behind.

Wildlife

Just as humans love peaches, so do most animals. Squirrels, possums, birds, rats and most insects relish the sticky, juicy fruit.

Medicinal Uses

Peach fruits are rich in antioxidants (the plant compounds that help your body fight against infection and diseases), as well as vitamins and minerals. Also, fresh peach juice and flesh are believed to help prevent UV damage. The great herbalist Culpepper, who died in 1541, suggested that peach juice would "clear and strengthen the lungs, and relieve those who vomit and spit blood". An infusion of dried peach leaves was once used to expel worms from the body.

PEACH MELBA

Fresh peach lends itself well to a kefir (see page 120). Here, though, in view of the enigmatic connection between trees and music, I'm offering a simple peach melba, a dessert named in honour of the Australian opera singer Dame Nelly Melba, who was the Lady Gaga of her day. The French chef Escoffier designed the dish specifically for her. Its simplicity shows you just how little is needed to produce something sublime.

Makes 6 servings (or 3 if you have greedy guests)

You will need:

6 peaches, perfectly ripe

1 tbsp caster (superfine) sugar, plus extra for sprinkling

about 20 ripe raspberries

12 large scoops of the best vanilla ice cream you can get your hands on

1. Boil a medium pan of hot water, keeping a pan of iced water within reach. Place the peaches, one at a time, into the hot water for 20 seconds, submerging the entire fruit.

2. Using a slotted spoon, lift the peach out of the hot water and plunge into the cold water. Repeat with the other 5 peaches. The skin will slide easily from the fruits. Put the skins in the compost bin.

3. Sprinkle the peaches all over with sugar, then pop into the fridge for 1 hour.

4. While waiting, purée the raspberries through a fine sieve to remove as many of the tiny pips as you can. Add the 1 tablespoon of sugar and stir.

5. To serve, put 2 large scoops of ice cream into each bowl, top with the peaches, then drizzle the raspberry sauce on top. Serve immediately.

PEACH FACE MASK

There are several compounds in a peach that make a rejuvenating face mask for both sexes. These include vitamin E, which perks up tired skin wonderfully, as well as potassium, which helps hydrate and moisturize. What's more, if you make your own face mask, you don't need to worry about the bewildering array of chemicals found in many over-the-counter products. Here, you're using just two ingredients – a peach and room-temperature plain yoghurt (which soothes and tightens the skin at the same time).

Cut a peach in half, remove the stone, and drop one half into boiling water for a few seconds; pour over cold water to remove the skin. Mash the de-skinned peach half with a fork, making it as smooth as you can. Add a teaspoonful of yoghurt and blend.

Apply the mask with your fingers and leave on for 20 minutes. Wash away with water and dry your face gently.

Your skin will feel soft and look glowing. All you have to do now is eat the other half of the peach.

Pear

Pyrus communis (RIGHT)
and *Pyrus pyrifolia*

**Song: "The Necklace of Wrens"
by The Gloaming**

Although apples and pears are often grouped together, there's a distinct feeling that the pear is the poor relative, which really isn't fair. For example, W B Yeats, in "The Song of the Wondering Aengus", writes lyrically of the "silver apples of the moon, the golden apples of the sun". But why didn't he include the pear in the poem? Why, when something goes wrong, do the English say it goes "pear-shaped"? There are several potential explanations for this odd description, but perhaps the forerunner is that it has its origins as a slang expression in the British Royal Air Force, which was used to describe pilots' less than perfect attempts at forming a circle when looping the loop.

It's thought that the pear originated in the Caucasus Mountains and spread to Asia and Europe. One of the oldest of all the cultivated trees, the pear tree was worshipped by the Chechen people. They believed that benevolent spirits inhabited both the pear and walnut trees and it was considered a terrible crime to chop them down for any reason.

Although, in my foraging adventures, I've seen lots of different sorts of crab apples and various wildings, I had never seen anything close to a "wild" pear until earlier this year. I'd stopped off at a friend's house, and we ended up going for a walk near a river with skimpy woodland. Through the trees I spotted what looked like an abandoned cottage. This is a rural area where the sight of tumble-down dwellings isn't uncommon, but it's always a thrill to clamber over old walls and work out what the house might have looked like. Which is exactly what we did. Once the roof is off a building (usually taken by locals for repurposing), stone houses fall apart pretty quickly, and this little place was no exception. I walked round the back of the house and right there was a small, happy-looking tree, which I assumed was an apple wilding. However, when I bit into one of the small fruits, there was no doubt that I was eating a pear – it was soft inside and delicious. Whether you consider yourself to be

What does it look like?

Growing to a height of 15m (49ft) and with a spread of 12m (39ft), the common pear is a tall, narrow shape. It is deciduous, with dark grey bark that cracks into small "tiles" in older specimens. The leaves are alternate and broad, oval in shape and up to 10cm (4in) in length. These leaves are hairy when young, becoming smoother with age. They are a glossy dark green on top, with fine "teeth" and a pointed tip. The white clustering flowers are 2.5cm (1in) wide, clothing the tree in exuberant white flounces in the summer (the common pear, in full blossom, looks very much like an overdressed and over excited old lady). The fruits that follow are – if you weren't sure before – distinctly pear-shaped. The common pear is only ever seen in cultivation, although there is a wild specimen, too – its parent. The wild pear is taller, growing up to 20m (66ft) tall. It can be found in wooded areas in various parts of Europe.

Pyrus communis "Bartlett"

a forager or not, a find like this is a huge thrill. Who needs caskets of doubloons when you can find a treasure like this little pear?

And this little pear wilding was part of a story, too – a remnant from the days when Herefordshire (where we did the walk) and its neighbouring counties Worcestershire and Gloucestershire were famed for their perry, a sweet alcoholic drink made from fermented pears, as well as for their apple cider. It seems that perry pears will grow in places where apple trees will not, and that the climatic conditions in these three counties are perfect for both fruits.

There used to be dozens of varieties of perry pears, many of them named for people and places (for example, Judge Amphlett and Bosbury Scarlet) and others that describe something about the tree or the nature of the fruit (Flakey Bark, Strawberry Pear) and still others (Sweet Huffcap, Tettenhall Dick, Zealous Wick) ... well, who knows? Here and there, tucked away in orchards or hidden away at the edges of woodlands, there are hybrids of these delightful fruity curiosities just waiting for a keen forager to find them. You might also like the grainy, floral flavour of the Chinese or Nashi pear (*Pyrus pyrifolia*), which is round like an apple and has a higher water content than the common pear.

Wildlife

Pears are enjoyed by lots of different birds, including thrushes and blackbirds, and the flowers are a good food source for bees. The foliage of a pear tree provides shelter for caterpillars, including that of the emperor moth.

Medicinal Uses

Although the apple is renowned as the fruit that keeps us healthy ("An apple a day keeps the doctor away"), not a lot of people know that the pear is the richer in minerals of the two fruits. They are neck and neck as regards content of sodium, potassium and phosphorous; however, the pear contains greater amounts of calcium, magnesium, iron, copper and zinc. As a medicine, pear is eaten to alleviate indigestion, constipation, nausea and vomiting.

PEAR CHUTNEY

A chutney is an Indian condiment, a blend of sweet, sour and spicy flavours. Underripe fruit is perfect in a chutney.

Makes 6 jars

You will need:

900g (2lb) firm pears, cored and sliced (I keep the peel on)

680g (1lb 8oz) red onions, peeled and chopped

2 large garlic cloves, peeled and crushed

150g (5½oz/1 cup) dried apricots, chopped

400g (14oz/2 cups) soft light brown sugar

1 tsp ground cumin

1 tsp ground coriander

1 tsp ground cinnamon

½ tsp cayenne pepper

70ml (2¼fl oz/4½ tbsp) apple cider vinegar

160g (5¾oz/⅔ cup) tomato puree (tomato paste)

6 x 300ml (10½oz) jars, sterilized

1. Put the pears and onions into a large, heavy-bottomed pan. Cook over a medium heat, stirring occasionally for around 15 minutes.

2. Add the rest of the ingredients and bring to the boil, then cover, turn down the heat and simmer for up to 2 hours, tasting for the consistency you want.

3. Pour into warmed, sterilized jars and seal when cool.

SPICED POACHED PEAR WITH ELDERBERRY

This is my take on a traditional pear dessert.

Makes 6 servings

You will need:

6 ripe pears

750ml (26fl oz/3¼ cups) Elderberry Winter Tonic (see page 63)

1 cinnamon stick

3 cloves

1 star anise

6 cardamom pods

A 2cm (1in) chunk of ginger

2 tbsp of apple juice (optional)

Ice cream or yoghurt, to serve

1. Peel the pears, leaving the stem on.

2. Put them into a pan, pour over the elderberry remedy and top up with water to cover the pears.

3. Add the spices and cook over a low heat for a couple of hours with the lid on, ladling the liquid over the pears from time to time so that they cook evenly. Top up with water as necessary – don't let it dry up.

4. Let cool, remove the spices, then use the stem of the pear to lift it from the pan. Serve with ice cream or thick creamy yoghurt. The dishes will hardly need washing.

DEHYDRATED PEAR SLICES

You can dehydrate pears in exactly the same way as apples – see page 17.

Plum

Prunus domestica (ABOVE) and *Prunis salicina*

**Song: "I Had Too Much To Dream Last Night"
by The Electric Prunes**

Not too far from where I live is the Worcestershire town of Pershore.
This place is said to be the plum capital of the UK, as it has its own
Festival of Plums, which is advertised as "The Largest Plum Show
on Earth". Pershore even has its own Plum Charmer. You'd think that
such a job would belong in the Middle Ages rather than the present
day, but this isn't the case. Part of the job of the Plum Charmer is
to "wake up" the fruit a few weeks before they're due to ripen and,
interestingly, the current Plum Charmer plays music to the fruits.

Prunus domestica

The idea is that the plums respond to music and the water molecules vibrate inside the fruit, encouraging the ripening process.

Once again, we look to the Caucasus region and Iran to find the origins of this tree. The two most commonly grown around the world are *Prunus domestica* and the Japanese plum, *Prunus salicina*. The plum trees you are most likely to find as a forager are the ones best treated as feral trees, which Richard Mabey describes as "one of the best wild foods (many being edible straight from the tree, unlike sloes) and representing a huge genetic reservoir". Often planted as quick-growing windbreaks to protect young orchards, these guardian trees hybridized

What does it look like?

The plum tree is part of the wider Prunaceae family, which includes a number of similar trees, such as apricot (*Prunus armeniaca*), wild cherry (*Prunus avium*), cherry plum (*Prunus cerasifera*), almond (*Prunus dulcis*), bullace or damson (*Prunus institia*), peach (*Prunus persica*), greengage subspecies (which is also called *Prunus domestica*), as well as the blackthorn (*Prunus spinosa*). All these are edible; however, be aware that the leaves and pits contain a miniscule amount of cyanide, hence the almond scent and flavour of the flowers.

The plum tree grows to a height of 10m (33ft), with a similar spread. It is deciduous, with suckers springing from the base of the young trees. Its matte green leaves are shaped a little like a footprint – widest toward the end and up to 8cm (3¼in) long. Plum tree bark is grey-brown in naturally, providing fortunate locals with an abundant crop of fruits with which to make jams, wines, fruit butters and liqueurs. The recipe for Fermented Cherries (see page 51) works really well for plums, too.

Plum's heartwood can provide a range of different shades, which become even more colourful with polishing. The cherry plum, in particular, has a lovely brownish red hue, the same shade as its leaves. Because the trunk of the tree is quite small and tends toward an irregular growth pattern, it is used for smaller items such as parts of musical instruments, knife handles and so on

Wildlife

Birds, including thrushes, blackbirds and jays, love to feast on soft or windfall plums. Mammals – such as squirrels, foxes, rats and mice – also like to eat the very ripe, squashy fruits. The open flowers attract butterflies and moths, such as the willow beauty.

colour, developing fissures as the tree ages. The small white (or pink) five-petalled flowers appear before the leaves unfurl. This characteristic – the leaves appearing at the same time or just after the blossoms – is common to most of the species; it's almost as though the blossoms can't wait to get going, hence the symbol of the tree as a sign of hope, a harbinger of spring. Take a walk in late winter or early spring, before any leaves are starting to show, and make a note of any white blossom you happen to see. Return to the tree later, when the fruits will give you the best indication of what you have found. The fruits of the different plum trees vary in colour, depending on the species: red, yellow, green and – my favourite – purple. The skin often has a "bloom", a waxy, whitish coating that protects the fruit by allowing it to regulate its own water content.

Medicinal Uses

There are over 200 species of plum, which contribute to a huge array of medicines. The most widely known is probably prune juice, made from naturally dried plums and used as a cure for constipation. Plums contain vitamin C and antioxidants that boost immunity.

MAKING CHARCOAL

Hard woods, such as ash, oak, hazel, apple and other fruit woods make the best charcoal. However, whatever hardwood you use needs to be seasoned in a dry, airy outdoor place for up to a year. I've found that people often prune their plum trees and simply burn the wood. You might want to use it to make charcoal, for drawing, instead. Just remember where you put the wood to season and make a note to remind yourself when it will be ready.

You will need:

A small steel container, such as a biscuit (cookie) tin, with a slightly loose lid (so it won't explode)

Seasoned hardwood stems, roughly the same size, which will fit in the tin

A firepit in which to burn the wood

Tongs, to lift the hot tin out of the ground

1. Make a hole in the side of the tin so that the fire has somewhere to go.
2. Build a fire – a fire pit is much the easiest option.
3. Fill the container with the wood, put the lid on loosely and use the tongs to put it on the burning fire.
4. Keep an eye on the container. You will see white smoke pouring out of the gap in the loose lid – this is fine. Have a look at the container from time to time.

5. When no more smoke or gas is coming out of the gap in the lid, use the tongs once more to carefully remove the hot tin from the fire and place on a fire-proof surface (such as a paving slab).
6. Allow the tin to cool completely before opening. Your charcoal should emerge as long sticks, which you can use for drawing, thereby joining the millions of human beings who have used charcoal to make drawings in caves or on walls as part of a process of getting to understand themselves.

Note that the natural process of making charcoal doesn't always run perfectly, so if your first attempt isn't up to scratch, do try again.

YUMMY PLUMMY LUNCHBOX TREAT

This recipe uses dates and coconut rather than sugar, so it's a healthy treat option. Keeps in the fridge for 10 days or so.
Makes 8–10 portions

You will need:
1kg (2lb 4oz) ripe plums, de-stoned and halved
50g (1¾oz) dates, de-stoned and chopped into small pieces
50g (1¾oz/⅔ cup) desiccated (dried shredded) coconut
50g (1¾oz) flaked (sliced) almonds, toasted (optional)
½ tsp ground cinnamon
½ lemon, plus more to squeeze
Toasted oats, for sprinkling

1. Pop the plums into a heavy-bottomed pan. Add all the other ingredients, except for the toasted oats, along with 3½ tablespoons water. Bring to the boil, then reduce the heat and let simmer for about 30 minutes.
2. Take off the heat and let cool completely.
3. Scoop into small jars and top with a sprinkle of toasted oats as a lunchbox treat or used on toast at breakfast time.

Quince

Cydonia oblonga (ABOVE) and *Chaenomeles japonica*

Album: "The Dude" by Quincy Jones

Made famous by the Edward Lear poem, the quince, along with mince, is what the Owl and the Pussycat ate when they set out to sea.

Apart from warding off the "evil eye" (as described by Pliny the Elder), according to the ancient Greeks and Romans, the quince fruit was sacred to Aphrodite and Venus, their respective goddesses of love. Accordingly, once upon a time, brides and grooms were offered a quince to share (although, as the fruit is so hard, it must have taken some effort to eat).

Native to central and south-west Asia, the quince has naturalized in lots of Mediterranean areas, although the majority of the quinces of the world are grown and harvested in China and Turkey. Despite liking the heat, they also need a period of colder weather for the flowers – and therefore the fruit – to form. The quince grows happily in the UK, where, along with the medlar and the mulberry, it makes up a trio of trees that were fashionable at the same time as wandering minstrels, the plague and the beheading of wives. Happily, all these trees are still present today, as long as you know where to look. In Britain this tends to be in the orchards of large gardens. I've made quite a few friends by offering to relieve people of quinces, and you might want to try this yourself; so many of them go to waste because people don't have the time to use them. This is a very strategic way of foraging.

In the 18th-century colonies of New England, it was the tradition to plant a quince at the lower end of the vegetable garden. I think this might be a throw-back to the time when early apple stems, used for grafting, were kept fresh on their long journeys from Kazakhstan by being pushed into the moisture-retentive quinces. The presence of quince trees may also have helped in pollination. Also, I'm reminded of the Chinese habit of planting a plum in a certain position as a protective influence. Perhaps there is always a practical reason in such old practices, as well as a comforting, superstitious one. Quince is rich in pectin, an effective setting agent for other jams and jellies. It also can be made into an utterly delicious florally fragrant jelly. However, as commercial pectin and gelatin developed, the quince tree – whose fruits are very hard to eat raw without breaking your teeth – fell out of favour. Quinces are still commercially grown in California, so it is here that you are most likely to find them naturalized in the wild.

If all this has left you longing to try this fruit but you're hampered by the lack of quince trees in your area, don't worry. You can cheat. The ornamental quince, or Chaenomeles, is one of those garden shrubs that lots of people have without realizing the astounding potential of its fruit, which does everything that its bigger cousin can do. It replicates by sending out suckers, and I've seen it growing wild in the UK as well as in Spain and Greece. The word "ornamental" can be really off-putting as a description of plants, as it gives you the idea that it is only for looking at, not for eating. The ornamental quince is generally grown for its cheery orange-red flowers, not its fruits, which most people don't know about. These miniature versions of the ones on the trees are round and knobbly, shaped either like an apple or a pear and are a little smaller than the size of a ping-pong ball. The fruits are set directly onto the spiny tangle of branches, with no stem at all. Sometimes when you pick them you will need to cut out a bit of woody stem that the fruit has grown around. Owners of these plants are generally happy to let you help yourself; pick them in the autumn and be sure to share whatever you make with them with your benefactor.

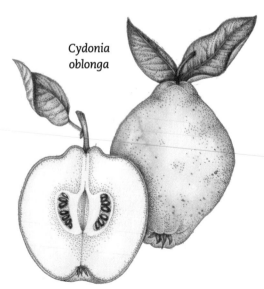

Cydonia oblonga

Wildlife

Quince flowers, particularly the open blossoms of the ornamental Japanese quince (*Chaenomeles japonica*), attract many pollinators, such as bees and butterflies.

Medicinal Uses

Quince has traditionally been made into a syrup to help a queasy stomach and combat looseness of the bowels. Up until the early 20th century, the seeds, which become

What does it look like?

The quince is a deciduous tree, growing to a height of 8m (26ft) with a similar spread. Its bark is a purple-brown colour, and flakes with age. The young shoots are covered with white hairs, becoming smooth and bald later on. Rounded or ovoid, its leaves are quite large at 10cm (4in) long and have short stems and smooth edges without teeth. Like the shoots, the leaves start out hairy. Their upper surface becomes smooth and is dark green on top, but they retain grey-white hairs underneath. Quince flowers consist of five white petals that are borne singly, and they blossom in late spring. The fruits appear in the autumn, either shaped like a lumpier version of an apple or a pear, and initially covered with woolly white hair that falls off as the fruits grow.

mucilaginous when boiled, were taken internally for conditions as wide-ranging as candida, dysentery and gonorrhoea. Latterly, quince has been used to ease morning sickness, hay fever and stomach ulcers. Quince also has antioxidant and antibacterial properties, which help fight infection and strengthen the immune system.

QUINCE PETIT FOURS

Quince Jelly or *membrillo* is delicious eaten with a good Manchego – a sheep's milk cheese from Spain, where together they form a very popular snack.

However, it is equally scrummy when turned into a sweet to eat with a small cup of black coffee. Cut the quince jelly into 3cm (1¼in) squares, and push an almond, half a cherry, a sliver of marzipan or whatever else you fancy into the top.

MEMBRILLO OR QUINCE JELLY

Makes 4 jars

You will need:

2kg (4lb 8oz) quince or
   ornamental quince fruits,
   washed, cored, de-pipped
   and chopped
1 vanilla pod
Juice and zest of 1 unwaxed
   lemon

About 1kg (2lb 4oz/5 cups)
   caster sugar (exact amount
   revealed during cooking –
   see step 3)
4 x 450g (1lb) glass jars,
   sterilized

1. Line a baking tray with greaseproof paper.
2. Put all the ingredients except the sugar into a large heavy-bottomed pan and cook until the quinces are soft and your kitchen smells like perfume.
3. Remove the vanilla pod and let the contents of the pan cool. Pick out any stray pips, then weigh the mixture. Add the same weight of sugar.
4. Put the mixture back into the pan and stir carefully over a low heat (the contents of the pan can "spit" as it gets hotter, so be warned). Leave to cook on a low heat, stirring from time to time, for up to 90 minutes. The colour will change from pale yellow to a rich brown. Allow to cool and pour into the warm sterilized jars and seal. Alternatively, pour the mixture into shallow trays and, when set, slice into squares. Wrap nicely in greaseproof (waxed) paper and you'll find that Christmas is sorted.

Rowan

Sorbus aucuparia

Song: "Magic Tree and I Let Myself Go" by Craig Armstrong, featuring Lana Del Ray

Rowan has some interesting hybrids, including a tree called *Sorbus leyana* or Ley's whitebeam, which is thought to have originated from a rowan crossed with a grey whitebeam. It is one of the rarest trees in the world. I knew that the only place it grows is in the Welsh valleys, but I didn't know exactly where. At one time I was leading a foraging walk through an ancient industrial landscape (which I mention in the chapter about Fig – see page 65). I was helping people to find wild plants and chatting along the way, when I was suddenly stopped in my tracks. There, along the limestone escarpment at head height and within touching distance, were not just one but 17 of these extremely rare trees. Incredible! I halted the walk to tell everyone what I knew: that this was one of the world's rarest trees, its known locations had been noted, but the place where we were was definitely not listed. I went on to explain how the tree needed specific conditions in which to grow, with open land in front and rocks to shelter it behind, and how it reproduces itself by cloning, not pollination. The icing on the cake was that the trees were covered in gorgeous red berries! I could see that most people were as thrilled as I was. Did anyone have any questions, I asked. A hand went up at the back. "Can we eat them?"

One of the alternative names for the rowan is the mountain ash. This might lead you to suppose that it is related to the ash tree (see page 19), but no. It's simply so-named because the leaves grow in the same pattern as those of the ash. If you're new to foraging, you could also confuse the blossoms of rowan with those of elderflower. However, heads of elder blossom are quite airy, whereas those of the rowan are tighter, more compact. Elderberries, when ripe, are small and black, whereas rowan berries are either red, or maybe a reddish brown, and significantly larger.

In the old mining areas in the Welsh valleys, not far from where I live, there's a town called Mountain Ash, named for the proliferation of the rowan trees that grow there. It's also the name of an area of Kentucky. It wasn't uncommon for miners from Wales to travel to the USA to share their expertise in wrenching coal from the bowels of the earth, so it's possible this town was named by the homesick miners who travelled all that way from Mountain Ash in Wales.

What does it look like?

The rowan tree grows to a height of 15m (49ft), with a spread of 10m (33ft). Its bark is glossy grey and smooth, forming ridges in older trees. The leaves are pinnate – arranged down the sides of a stem. In this case there are up to 15 sharply toothed, tapering leaflets, which are dark green on top and a blue-green underneath. Each leaf grows up to 20cm (8in) long. The clusters of small, creamy white flowers, each with five petals, appear in late spring followed by neat bundles of rowan berries that tend to weigh down the tree's branches.

Until not long ago, I lived halfway up a mountain in South Wales, in the UK. I was surrounded by rowan trees, which seemed to relish the harsh winters and hot summers. Although the rowan originates in Europe and the Western part of Asia, different species of them grow happily anywhere with a temperate climate, including in parts of the USA, where it has naturalized comfortably since it was brought from Europe.

Sorbus aucuparia

The trees that surrounded my home, as I now know, were of the species *Sorbus aucuparia*. Since there were so many of them, I started to look into the folklore of the tree. And I found that as far as it goes, "my" rowan seems to be quite contradictory.

I'll give you an example. Although the tree is said to repel witches, it also grows where witches live. And for the druids (both ancient and modern) the tree acts as a sort of door or gateway (a bit like the Japanese sacred archway or *torii*) that can transport you into another world. If you're a druid who likes to make wine, you may be interested to know that drinking rowan wine – in a ritual way rather than just as a means of getting jolly – was traditionally believed to enable druids to see into the future – so, it also offered a different sort of portal. Or maybe it was just the alcohol content that worked the magic? I'll leave you to decide.

According to British folklore, the rowan is an "atropaic" plant. This means it is believed to ward off evil or pernicious influences. This handy tree repels the "evil eye", curses, dark magic including psychic attacks, and keeps your house safe from bursting into flames. Tell your insurance company that you are protected by a rowan tree near your back door and see what they say.

Wildlife

The caterpillars of the apple fruit moth feed on the fruits, as do many birds including waxwings, thrushes, redstarts and fieldfares. The blossoms attract bees, butterflies and other pollinators, including the peacock butterfly and the apple fruit moth.

Medicinal Uses

Traditionally, rowan berries – which are rich in vitamin C – were used to relieve scurvy, a disease that isn't as prevalent as it once was. The symptoms of scurvy included general weakness, soreness in the limbs and even bleeding skin. Vitamin C is a very effective cure for this disease. The berries are also high in fibre and contain antioxidants. These are compounds that help protect the body against various ailments, including cancer, by stimulating the production of the white blood cells that destroy disease-causing pathogens. Sorbic acid – named after the tree – is used as a food preservative since it inhibits the growth of various toxic bacteria, including *Clostridium botulinum*, which can be fatal to humans.

ROWAN WINE

I wanted to make this wine as the ancient druids would have drunk it. It works well as a full-bodied and tasty wine, although I'm not entirely certain whether it made me see into the future. In fact, after drinking it, I couldn't remember anything at all.

Makes 6 bottles

You will need:

1.3kg (3lb) rowan berries
4.5l (1 gallon) boiling water
450g (1lb/3¼ cups) raisins, chopped
1.3kg (3lb/6½ cups) sugar

2 apples, chopped
1 tbsp citric acid
1 tsp wine yeast or 1 slice sourdough toast
1 tsp yeast nutrient

A very large food-grade
  container with lid
A demijohn with an airlock

6 x 70cl (24fl oz) glass bottles
  with screw tops

1. Put the berries in the large container and pour the boiling water over them. Leave for 3 days.
2. Sieve the berries through a muslin (cheesecloth) or plastic sieve, retaining as much of the pulp as possible.
3. Stir in the raisins, sugar, apples, citric acid and yeast. Mix well, put the lid on tight and leave to ferment in a warm place for 2 weeks.
4. Sieve the liquid into the demijohn and add the airlock.
5. Leave until the solids have settled and the fizzing has stopped.
6. Pour into bottles, seal and store in a cool place. Drink when you're ready.

ROWAN PROTECTIVE AMULET

Rowan was traditionally made into a protective amulet. It was hung over the crib of a newborn infant to stop the child being taken away by a witch in exchange for a "changeling" – a fairy child who, unlike the human it was traded in for, had very bad manners and was impossible to control. If you have pesky family members, consider whether this might have happened to them.

While you might not be worried about witches invading your home these days, you can follow in this tradition by making your own protective rowan amulet. Simply find two sticks of rowan wood of similar girth, one longer than the other, and make them into a cross by binding them together with red thread. You can hang a large version above your front door or elsewhere in your home or carry a smaller, portable amulet in your pocket as a charm.

Sea Buckthorn

Hippophae rhamnoides

Song: "White Feather" by The Girl in the Tree House

The name of this tree is said to have come from the ancient Greeks, who occasionally fed their horses on the leaves and noticed that the animals' manes looked shiny and healthy after eating them. *Hippo* means "horse" in Greek and *phaos* means "to shine" or "shining".

Sea buckthorn was introduced into the US in the 1920s. I have a confession to make. I live in a mountainous region, with no sea buckthorn to be had for miles and miles, and so, until recently, I had never seen the actual tree. My birthday is in August and last year I asked for the gift of a trip to the coast to search for sea buckthorn.

What does it look like?

The sea buckthorn may well prove the most elusive of all the trees in this book. Also called the "seaberry", "sandthorn" or "sallowthorn", the name tells you that this is a coastal plant. Deciduous, it grows to a height of up to 10m (33ft), forming thickets that have a spread of 6m (20ft). It grows quite prolifically, spreading by suckers from its base. The bark is a brownish-black colour, with fissures developing as the tree ages. Its leaves grow up to 7cm (2¾in) long and they alternate. Lance-shaped, they are covered in silvery scales on both their upper side and underside. In spring small yellowish flowers appear either before the leaves or at the same time. After the flowers come the fruits, bright orange and fleshy, clustered densely along the shoots. Although the sea buckthorn is seen as a wild plant, it is often grown deliberately to hold sand dunes together, as well as to make a dense barrier wherever it might be needed. It is very hardy and can withstand temperatures of -43°C (-45°F).

As soon as I saw the tree, I knew what it was. This is where reading about trees, and looking at images of them, comes in handy. I also knew it's the berries that you want and that they're notoriously meddlesome to gather, as they're naturally squishy and grow on thorny branches. But it was worth it – the flavour was as lovely and as interesting as I had expected, like a mixture of mango, lemon and sour orange, with maybe a hit of pineapple. However, the real thrill for me was seeing a tree that I had only previously ever seen in books – it was like meeting an old friend. I hope you feel like this about some of the trees I've included in this book.

Since I'm a newbie to sea buckthorn, I asked my colleagues in the Association of Foragers to let me use some of their recipes.

I've found that the foraging community all over the world loves sharing ideas, recipes and locations.

Hippophae rhamnoides

Wildlife

The fruits are eaten by a number of birds, including fieldfares, and the leaves provide fodder for butterfly and moth caterpillars, such as the emperor moth.

Medicinal Uses

To date, there have been no clinical trials for sea buckthorn. However, in the countries where it originates, such as Mongolia, China, Russia, Canada and parts of Europe, traditional uses include using extracts of the leaves and flowers as a cure for arthritis and gout. The oil can be applied directly to soothe sunburned skin. Sea buckthorn berries could be called a superfood, as they contain the entire array of fatty acids, including heart-protecting Omega 3, 6, 7 and 9 and many beneficial vitamins and minerals, such as vitamins C and E and magnesium and calcium.

SEA BUCKTHORN POSSET
by Lisa Cutliffe of Edulis Wild Food
Makes 4 little pots

You will need:
300ml (10½fl oz/1¼ cups) double (heavy) cream
75g (2½oz/⅓ cup) caster (superfine) sugar

100ml (3½fl oz/scant ½ cup) sea buckthorn juice

1. Put the cream and sugar into a heavy-bottomed pan and bring to the boil.
2. Take off the heat, let it cool, then add the sea buckthorn juice.
3. Once fully cool, pop into the fridge for a couple of hours to set.

Lisa also suggests adding something to give the posset a little crunch – for example, snappy biscuits or smashed-up hazelnuts.

SEA BUCKTHORN MARMALADE
by Andy Knott of Wild Food Dorset
Makes 4 jars

You will need:

500g (1lb 2oz) sea buckthorn pulp and juice
500g (1lb 2oz/2½ cups) jam sugar
1 small apple, peeled and diced
1 tbsp ground cinnamon
Juice of 1 lemon
4 x 320ml (10¾oz) jars, sterilized

1. If you don't have a jam thermometer, pop a saucer into the freezer. (You'll need this later to see if your marmalade has set).
2. Put the sea buckthorn into a heavy-bottomed pan and stew for about 15 minutes at a low temperature.
3. Add the sugar, diced apple, cinnamon and lemon juice, and bring to the boil.
4. If using a thermometer, once your marmalade has reached a temperature of 104°C (219°F) let it cool a little. If you don't have a thermometer, use the cold saucer test. Take the saucer from the fridge, add a small dollop of the marmalade and leave for a minute or so. If the marmalade wrinkles when you touch it, it is ready.
5. Pour into the warm, sterilized jars and seal.

Sumac

Rhus typhina

Song: "Le Jardin de Lucy" by Sumac Dub

I'm very fond of the sumac. It's another one of those plants whose beauty is often hidden in plain view, especially since it is so tenacious – it sends out suckers left, right and centre until people regard it as a pest and no longer admire its ability to grow just about anywhere. It's safe to say that if you have a sumac, you will never lose it!

Although this tree is native to the USA as well as Africa, the Middle East and the Mediterranean regions, it's likely there is one close to where you live, wherever you are – only you just can't see it.

What does it look like?

A spreading tree, the sumac often has a shrubby appearance because it throws up lots of suckers from around its base. Its average optimum height and spread are both around 10m (33ft). The leaves are alternately pinnate with up to 27 leaflets, which are dark green on the top and greeny blue underneath. These leaflets measure up to 10cm (4in) in length and are borne on stems that can grow up to 60cm (1ft 11in) long. The bark is a deep brown colour, and smooth. In late summer to early autumn, the tiny green flowers carried in dense conical clusters turn a bright red and when the red fruit appear each is matted to the next with long hairs. The sight of these red "bobs" or cones sitting erect on the tree is very cheery. The berries are in fact a drupe – a cluster of individual bobbles, each holding a seed within it.

For example, just around the corner from where I live in rural Wales, there's a lovely sumac leaning over the wall of a little-used holiday cottage. This is very handy for me as no one cares if I harvest the bobs to use – they don't know what they're missing. I've spotted the sumac equally at home on a swanky roof terrace in London as growing on the wasteland alongside railway tracks like a colourful interloper.

Sumac uses are as many and varied as the countries it hails from. The *Rhus coriaria* variety, also known as Tanners' sumac, provides the rich red colouring for the slippers, bags and pouffes you might find in a Morrocan souk, whereas another variety, *Rhus verniciflua*, was at one time grown in Japan specifically to make candles. The one we are featuring here most, though, is *Rhus typhina* or stag's horn sumac, which is possibly the commonest and easiest to find. If you have ever had the opportunity to stroke the soft

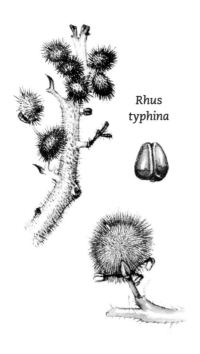

*Rhus
typhina*

muzzle of a stag or, better still, a reindeer, you'll get an idea of the smooth, furry texture of this particular variety.

Although the sumac grows prolifically in the UK, not many people are familiar with one of the folk names for the tree in the USA: the lemonade tree. (See recipe to find out why ...)

Wildlife

The berries are a favourite food of ring-necked pheasants, tufted grouse, crows, wild turkeys, the American robin and the European starling, among others. And the tree is an especially valuable food source for wildlife because the fruits stay on the branches into the colder months of the year. In the spring, honeybees and other pollinators are attracted to the flowers.

Medicinal Uses

In the USA, the Iroquois and Chippewa peoples traditionally had many uses for sumac. They used it to treat digestive problems, stomach aches, respiratory and reproductive problems as well as wounds from arrows. The berries were steeped in honey and strained to make a cough remedy, and the roots boiled up to make a tea that would induce vomiting when necessary. A decoction helped treat digestive upsets and similar ailments, and the powdered bark and berries are said to have been combined with a smoking mix for ceremonial use. We know that sumac berries are rich in antioxidants, which help protect the body from cell damage.

Because they also have anti-inflammatory properties, they may help prevent heart disease and cancer. In addition, indications suggest that sumac may be effective in managing the blood sugar levels of people with type-2 diabetes.

SUMAC LEMONADE

This is so simple and so delicious. You can add maple syrup or sugar if you want to, but I like the sharp, fizzy tartness of the sumac all on its own.

On a dry, sunny day, harvest a couple of fresh bobs and break them up over a tall jar so that you don't waste any of the flavour. Add 1 litre (35fl oz/4¼ cups) of water. Leave for a few hours, then strain the liquid through muslin (cheesecloth) into a jug to remove any hairy bits. Add ice and serve. It's as simple as that!

SUMAC SPICE

These fuzzy red clusters are where the sumac gets to be exciting. If you see one, provided the weather is dry, lick your finger and stroke the drupe. Then lick the same finger again. You'll get an acidic, lemony kick, sour and delicious. However, if you try the same trick after it has been raining, nothing will happen because the rain washes away the flavour until the drupe dries out again.

This delicious lemony flavour can be captured as a spice and mixed with sea salt, as used in Middle Eastern cooking. Gather three or four bobs on a sunny day and leave them to dry in a warm, ventilated room. Then, break apart all the tiny bobs and blitz them in a food processor. Sift them to remove any hard bits, then blitz them again, adding sea salt if you wish. You will end up with a coarse or fine powder, depending on how you like it.

Sweet Chestnut

Castanea sativa

Song: "Sweet Chestnut" by Kirsten Hanne

While I'm writing this book, I keep changing my mind about which of the trees I love the most. All sorts of memories keep popping up. And the image that's in my mind right now is of the street vendors selling chestnuts when I was a kid, just before Christmas when it was already dark by 4pm. After school we'd get the bus into town to the travelling fair. There were dodgems, hook-a-duck stalls and bags of candyfloss hanging everywhere. But my favourite was the chestnut seller, roasting the nuts on a brazier that spitted and sparked as he flipped the cooked nuts to the side of the pan.

I even liked the acrid smell of nuts that had been scorched beyond redemption, and especially loved the red hot paper cones of perfect chestnuts that you squeezed to crack open, nibbling on the little bits of soft, deliciously sweet, glossy chestnut kernels, even though they were really way too hot. It was a total sensory experience and a reminder of how good hot food tastes outdoors.

I hadn't seen chestnuts sold on the streets for years until I found myself in Florence the weekend before Christmas in 2019. It was the perfect time to be there. Best of all, though, I rounded a corner into a huge square, where a crowd of people were gathered around something or someone. I edged into the circle only to see the roast chestnut man – a real show off – tossing nuts into the air as he kept up a steady patter of jokes and fragments of song. The scent was just the same, and I became eight years old again, just for a moment.

The nuts of the American chestnut (*Castanea dentata*) were enjoyed by the native people for generations, certainly for a long time before the settlers arrived with their own chestnut species.

In 1904, though, chestnut blight was accidentally brought into the country and within 40 years the tree was virtually extinct. The American Chestnut Foundation is working toward reintroducing the tree by breeding varieties that are resistant to the blight.

The timber of the sweet chestnut tree is a hardwood, which means it's very durable. It's a popular wood for furniture, fencing and carving, and it is lighter than oak. The tannins of the tree are used to tan leather.

Wildlife

Red squirrels and mice love to eat sweet chestnuts, while bees and a number of other insects enjoy the nectar and pollen of the flowers. The leaves and nuts also provide a feast for micro-moths.

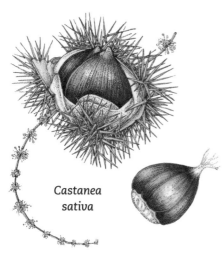

Castanea
sativa

Medicinal Uses

The leaves are used in traditional medicine in both Europe and the USA to cure whooping cough, bronchitis and respiratory ailments. There's evidence that this works, as the tree contains a compound that has expectorant properties. A tea made from the leaves of the sweet chestnut can be used to soothe mild asthma symptoms. The nuts are very nutritious as they are high in carbohydrates and B vitamins, and they are the only nuts that contain vitamin C, making them useful for those recovering from illness. Sweet chestnuts are gluten-free and are therefore a useful ingredient for people with coeliac disease.

What does it look like?

A sweet chestnut tree grows up to 30m (98ft) in height, with a spread of 20m (66ft). Its bark is smooth and purple-grey when young, developing distinctive, clockwise, spiralling ridges as it ages. The leaves are long and tapering with coarse-toothed edges; they are a deep glossy green on top and a lighter colour underneath. The flowering catkins are very noticeable – up to 25cm (10in) long, pale golden and fluffy. The fruits have a soft, spiny outer coating which, when they ripen in the autumn, split to reveal three glossy seeds inside. Usually, the largest of the three seeds is the best one to eat, as the others tend to be more skin than nutmeat. Unlike the casings of the horse chestnut, sweet chestnuts have

ROASTING CHESTNUTS

The absolute best way to eat chestnuts, by far, is exactly as I have described! You'll need to add in a crisp, starry winter's night, and, assuming that you don't have your own brazier, chestnuts that have been foraged by you in the afternoon, then split carefully with a sharp knife before being popped into a hot oven for 15 minutes. Put them on trays and bring them out to eat outdoors, watching for fireworks or maybe even shooting stars. Bliss.

CHESTNUT SWEDISH FIRE LOG – TWO WAYS

A Swedish fire log is a section of a tree trunk about half a metre (20in) high, with a good girth. For the first way to make one, you will need a chainsaw to cut a cross on the top of the log (as if you are cutting a cake into quarters) and then into eighths if possible, depending on the size of the log. (However, don't use a chainsaw unless you are trained or definitely know what you

a cute little tuft sticking out of the top, like Tintin's hair. This is called the "flame". Chestnut trees can live up to 1,000 years or more. If you find yourself in ancient woodland, keep your eyes peeled for signs of chestnut coppices – a telltale sign is a wide tree stump with chestnut branches shooting forth. If you're not sure how to tell the difference between the sweet chestnut and the horse chestnut (see page 80), compare the illustrations and note the many distinguishing features. Chestnut varieties can be found all over the world, as well as in the UK and the USA. You can see them in Europe, Malaysia, Japan, Korea, China – and in India, where they were introduced by the British colonists.

are doing. As I was told by a woodsman once, it's hard to stitch a hand back on.)

Next, saw deeper into the cross you have made, to about two thirds of the way down into the log. Then, push dried leaves, dried rotting wood, dried grasses, newspaper and other tinder into the space in the middle of the log, through the centre of the cuts. Now you can light the tinder – the log will burn for ages. If you need to leave it, douse it with water and make sure it has gone out completely.

The second way of making a fire log doesn't require a chainsaw, but you do need to find a dozen or so dry lengths of wood. Ideally, these should be a little thicker in girth than a rolling pin and roughly the same as a rolling pin in length (so you'll probably need to do a bit of sawing). The only other things you need are a length of garden wire and some tinder.

Bundle the logs together, stuffing dried grasses, leaves, paper or similar tinder into the bundles. Next, bind the logs together with the wire; you might need to do this in two or three places along your log bundle. Then, stuff more dried grasses into any other gaps between the logs. Set the log bundle vertically, making sure it is stable, for example a fire pit, and light the tinder. Just like the larger fire log described above, it will burn for ages.

If you can't find sweet chestnut wood, you can substitute any log of a suitable size that has been cut down, sliced into large chunks and left to dry out for a while.

Walnut

Juglans regia (ABOVE) and *Juglans nigra*

Song: "Redwood Tree" by Jamie Drake

When I was a little girl, walnut veneer was fashionable. Walnut timber is richly patterned with all sort of odd shapes, including weird forms and faces, and for a while it was all the rage to use this to advantage in making furniture. Sheets of veneer were split and glued together to make a mirror image. The walnut veneer wardrobe in my bedroom seemed, in my imagination, to show a portrait of Satan himself, a horned monster leering out from his wooden prison, which I found terrifying on summer evenings when I was sent to bed at 7pm and there were hours to go before it got dark.

What does it look like?

The common walnut (*Juglans regia*) reaches 18m (59ft) tall when fully grown and has a canopy of the same dimensions. The leaves are large, with 5–9 leaflets graduating in size growing on the same stem and reaching up to 45cm (18in) in length. Also called the English walnut because this is where it is mainly found, this deciduous tree has beautiful bark that is brown at first and melds into a distinctive grey as it ages. It is highly fissured and ideal for bark rubbings.

The black walnut (*Juglans nigra*), native to North America, grows to the same size. The leaves appear on stems up to 60cm (24in) long, with up to 23 leaflets arranged along the stem, rather like those of the ash. The bark has a diamond pattern, cracking deeply with age.

A good way to identify a walnut tree is to crush the leaves between your fingers. The scent it releases will remind you of furniture polish. An even easier way to establish that you're looking at a walnut tree is by the fruits. Both trees have similar-looking fruits: round green balls about the size of a ping-pong ball that split open when ripe, revealing the bumpy, wrinkly walnut shell. The creamy white walnut stays safe in its woody cocoon, waiting for you to make a mess of cracking it open, usually at Christmas.

Inside that shell are the two halves of the nut, which resemble a brain. You'll find a thin skin covering the "brain" bit, which is fine to eat, although a little bitter. If you want to remove it, pop the nut into hot water for 5 minutes or so, then rub it away.

Even when the fruits are not yet present on the tree, turning over leaf litter will reveal leaves, shell husks and other natural debris that are all part of the walnut's story. Left on the ground its green hulls start to rot, turning black and oozing an inky dark liquid that is impossible to remove from clothes and will stain your fingers for some time.

I did my best to stop falling asleep because I feared, if I did, the Devil would get me. And he was always still there in the morning.

Walnut trees are slow growing; if you're thinking of planting one, find a tree that has been grafted (usually with a black walnut), to make the wait for fruit a little shorter. Walnut trees don't like other plants to be close by, probably because of the growing space they need. There's an old saying: "nothing grows under a walnut tree".

The fable of the walnut tree is one of the stories that were either written or collected by the Greek storyteller, Aesop, who lived c.620–564 BC. Briefly, the story is about a walnut tree that stands innocently by a road. In trying to get the nuts down from the tree, people hurl rocks and stones at it; the tree observes, very astutely, that "People like to enjoy my fruits, but they have a very harsh way of showing how grateful they are". There's another ancient saying, passed down from the Romans, that mentions beating walnut trees to increase their fruit yield. I was quite surprised when friends of mine, who own what is effectively a walnut forest, confirmed that this does, indeed, make them more fruitful.

Wildlife
Mice, squirrels, racoons and other mammals relish them, too. Crows have been seen taking walnuts into their beaks, flying up into the air to a height of 20 metres (66 feet) or more, then dropping the nuts to crack the shells open. A number of moths and butterfly larvae rely on walnuts to provide food, including the brown-tail, small emperor and common emerald moths and the banded hairstreak butterfly.

Juglans regia

Medicinal Uses
Humankind has been eating walnuts since at least 7,000 years BC. The nuts were

revered as a food fit for the gods and dedicated to Jupiter, hence the *juglans* part of the name. The tree is traditionally associated with wisdom, the intellect, focus and clarity. In view of this, it's interesting to know that walnuts contain omega-3 fatty acids, which are beneficial for the joints, heart and brain, and also help boost memory. We usually get omega-3 fatty acids in our diets through eating oily fish, such as sardines. If you're vegan or vegetarian, try walnuts instead. How could we have known all this prior to clinical trials? Maybe it was pure coincidence, to do with the appearance of the nut, which really does look brain-like.

WALNUT INK

If you haven't made the oak gall ink on page 128, the recipe here is much less time-consuming, so is a good way to start. If you've ever seen the elaborate sketches and cartoons drawn by Leonardo da Vinci or Galileo, you will probably have noticed the lovely sepia-coloured ink. This is the ink that you are going to make (although it's unlikely that da Vinci would have had the benefit of a slow cooker).

First, find some walnuts that have fallen to the ground and started to rot. It doesn't take long for the fruits to go black.

You will need:

1kg (2lb 4oz) walnut hulls,
   rotten and black

Gum arabic (optional)

1 tsp iron/vinegar solution,
   optional (see pages 128–9)

Sieve, muslin (cheesecloth),
   coffee filter paper, for filtering

Funnel, for bottling

Small glass ink bottles

1. Put the walnut hulls into a slow cooker or pan, cover with water and simmer for about 6 hours, topping up the water as necessary.
2. Reduce the amount of liquid by simmering, with the lid off, until you have just 475ml (16½fl oz) left in the cooker or pan.

3. Let the liquid cool, then, using successively finer filters, remove any debris. Start with a fine-meshed sieve and, if you have the patience, end with muslin or coffee filter paper. It's worth spending time on this as the silkier the ink, the better your drawing or writing will look.
4. Add a few drops of gum arabic, if using. Try the ink and see what it looks like – if you'd like it to be darker, then add a few drops of the vinegar solution, if using.
5. Use the funnel to pour your ink into the little bottles. Store your walnut ink in a dark place to help the colour stay stable or transfer to a brown bottle.

LIGURIAN WALNUT PESTO

Pesto, you may or may not know, was "born" in Liguria. This recipe was adapted by my partner Liam for when we occasionally hold our pop-up restaurant, "1,000 Footsteps", which uses ingredients gathered within exactly one mile of wherever the venue is. One such area included walnuts, and this is what he devised.

Makes 6–8 generous dollops

You will need:

50g (1¾oz/heaped ½ cup) fresh walnuts, broken up

1 bunch wild garlic (ramsons), (roughly a handful) or 5 "tame" cloves

1 small bunch of fresh green herbs of your choice

Dollop of homemade yoghurt cheese or small piece of soft cheese, such as goat's cheese

Sea salt and freshly ground black pepper

2 tbsp walnut oil

Hosta leaf, to serve (optional)

1. Blend all the ingredients, except the oil, until your pesto is at the desired texture.
2. Stir in the walnut oil and serve in a hosta leaf (leaves and flowers are edible) if you can find one, or with fresh pasta, if not.

Willow

Salix alba (ABOVE), *Salix babylonica* and *Salix caprea*

Song: "Willow's Song" by Magnet

I'm very fond of a particular goat willow (*Salix caprea*) that
I occasionally check on. It's such a beautiful tree, quite small,
and one that's very easy to climb as the first branch is only a metre
and a half (about 5 feet) off the ground. Years ago, we were advised
that the tree didn't have long to live and that it might be best to
bring it down. This was really depressing, as we'd only just moved
into the house where this little willow took pride of place in the
meadow by the river. I mentioned this to a friend who was visiting.
She immediately drove into town and came back a couple of hours

later with a quantity of wide yellow ribbon, telling us that the tree was fine, all it needed was to know that it was loved. And, as in the song, she tied the yellow ribbon round the tree, ending with a floppy bow. We used to have a mini-music festival there and always hung labelled presents on the tree for the kids. They loved it, and it was the first tree that many of them ever climbed. The tree grew so well in the following years that the ribbon eventually snapped, but it's still going strong more than twenty years later, now covered in long cobwebby strands of lichen.

There are so many uses for willow. Because the wood is very hard and water-resistant, it was traditionally (and still is) used to make clogs, whose thick platform soles meant that their wearer (usually a peasant, in times past) would be able to keep their feet dry while working in the fields. The best cricket bats are made from willow polished with linseed oil. And if you're of a superstitious persuasion (and let's admit it, most of us are, even if just a bit), then you can keep a cross made of willow in a bowl of water to act as a "thunder charm" and keep your house safe from the ravages of storms.

Although there are many different natural materials used for weaving baskets and other containers, willow is probably the best-known. My little goat willow wouldn't be the best for this purpose, though; you need the kind that coppice readily and send out quick-growing shoots that are long, slim and flexible, such as the osier (Salix viminalis). Any material that can be woven is called "wicker", which means a "slender, pliable twig."

Wildlife

The nectar produced by abundant willow blossoms, which bloom in spring, provides a welcome feast for insects, particularly bees – listen out for their low, satisfied hum. Both birds and mammals use willow as a shelter. In addition, willow is a pioneer tree, perfect for re-establishing itself in land that has been damaged by overuse.

Medicinal Uses

Read this section, then see if you know the name of the medicine given to us by the willow. You may well be aware that the bark contains salicylates (hence the genus name *Salix*). What you might not know is that humans have used willow medicinally for at least 4,000 years, a practice adopted not only by the Sumerians but also the Chinese and ancient Greek civilizations, too. The Greek physician Dioscorides, writing in the 1st century AD, describes willow as having anti-inflammatory properties.

The question is this. How did we know which of the thousands of natural medicines would work, and for what ailment? The short answer is simple. Trial and error. I feel incredibly fortunate to be on the receiving end of generations of people desperately trying to find cures for all sorts of ailments, with not much more than guesswork,

What does it look like?

There are many types of willow, most of which you'll find close to water as they like to stand in ground that's damp. Perhaps the commonest one is the white willow (*Salix alba*), which grows to a height of 25m (82ft), with a spread of 20m (66ft). This is a deciduous tree, with drooping shoots. The leaves are long, lance-shaped and finely toothed, ending in a tapering point. They are silkily hairy when young and turn a dark green on top, blue-green underneath. The catkins – a delight of flower arrangers the world over – bear tiny flowers in the spring. The males are bright yellow in colour and the females, green. These are borne on separate trees, so two trees are needed to propagate. Possibly the best-known willow, though, is the weeping willow (*Salix babylonica*), whose long, pendulous shoots often trail mournfully into water.

Salix fragilis

and maybe the ancient Doctrine of Signatures, to help. The idea behind the Doctrine of Signatures is that if a part of a plant looks like a part of a body, then the plant in question might be useful in fixing the corresponding organ. Do you think this would work? Me, neither. But before science, all we were left with was guesswork and superstition. However, we do know that remedies that have been in continuous use are more likely to be "true".

In 1763 the first-ever clinical trial into the willow took place. The Reverend Edward Stone, an English cleric, studied the effect of willow bark powder on candidates suffering from the "ague" (which sounds a bit like flu) and found it to be "very efficacious."

And in 1828, Johann Buchner, a German pharmacologist, managed to isolate a yellow substance from the tannins of willow bark, which he called "salicin". Fast forward to 1895 and the German chemist Felix Hoffmann – who is generally credited with having "discovered" the drug – found a way of making it less harsh on the stomach. Hoffmann worked for the pharmaceutical company, Bayer, which still makes the drug. And yes, the drug is aspirin.

HOW TO DOWSE

Willow is one of the woods traditionally used in making a dowsing rod – a piece of wood either naturally or deliberately shaped like a Y, which is used for finding things, specifically water. This is an unusual technology and quite a controversial one. Some people swear by it. It seems that some people are natural dowsers, some not, but a friend of mine told me that anyone can dowse if they practise. There's only one way to find out.

The only things you need are a willow branch that is already shaped like a Y, or which can be split to make the letter's shape, and a friend to accompany you.

Find an open outdoor space and ask your friend to bury a small object an inch or so below the ground. As you're learning, restrict the area for burying the object so you're not still out there when night has fallen and the owls are hooting. DO NOT PEEK as your friend hides the object. When you're ready, lightly hold your rod at each end of the Y, with your thumb on the top and your forefinger below. Don't squeeze too hard, the rod needs to be able to move.

Clear your mind and, holding the rod out in front of you, slowly begin to pace the area. Don't try to "operate" the rod – just relax. If you're very lucky, the rod will find the object without you needing to do anything. If you don't succeed first time, try again.

If you can't find willow, hazel or witch hazel will also make a good dowsing rod.

WEAVE A WILLOW STAR

First, find a willow stick approximately 1.5m (5ft) long. Cut it, and strip off the leaves and side shoots. Make a bend in the willow about a third of the way along from the bottom of the stick.

Then make another bend, about 8cm (3¼in) long, followed by three more, all the same size. Now, you should have four kinks in the willow stick. Go back to the first two bends and form them into a triangle shape with the long part of the stick. Push the fourth kink through and shape into a star. You can increase the number of bends in the stick if you want a fuller, fatter star.

When I'm taking people on foraging walks, I show how to make these whenever I can find suitable long stems. Everyone loves them.

Witch Hazel

Hamamelis mollis and *Hamamelis virginiana* (ABOVE)

Song: "Witch Hazel" by Julia Rich

The botanical name of this tree, *Hamamelis*, comes from *hama* (Greek for "together") and *mela* ("fruit"), as the flowers and the fruit (which are what we call nuts) appear at the same time.

The whippy, forked branches of witch hazel were used by European colonists as well as Native Americans to search out water sources; if the endeavour was successful, this was called "witching a well", which turned into "wishing well" and, unsurprisingly, those who had an aptitude for dowsing were rumoured to have superhuman – or supernatural – powers. Witch hazel's original connection with witches is through the root of the word "witch", from the Middle English *wiche*, which means "to bend" or "be pliable". In this case it refers to the pliable branches of the tree.

Witch hazel was introduced to the UK at the turn of the 19th century. I didn't realize that the tree I passed occasionally by the gates of an abandoned quarry was a witch hazel until I saw it in the winter, some years ago now. I picked a couple of small branches that had flowers attached, thinking that the heady scent would make my little office smell less of damp border collies. Sadly, although the flowers smelled amazing outdoors, once I brought them inside, their scent was quite medicinal – a bit like antiseptic cream.

Wildlife

The tangled branches of witch hazel provide shelter for nesting birds in spring, and the scent of the flowers in winter is an important source of pollen during mild spells. The flowers are

What does it look like?

A deciduous tree reaching 5m (16ft) in both height and spread, the witch hazel is a curious-looking plant, which is native to the USA. The leaves are quite long, up to 15cm (6in) in length, with leaves that resemble those of a hazel (although the tree is not related to the hazel tree). The flowers, which appear in the winter after the leaves have fallen, are yellow and quite unlike any other flower I've ever seen. Thin, waving and twisting red or yellow tendrils, in groups of four, emerge from short stems along the branches. These flowers are followed by black seeds, which are edible and taste like a cross between hazelnuts and pistachios. However, it's unlikely that you will be lucky enough to try them since as soon as they're ripe they burst, flinging themselves to a distance of approximately 6m (20ft). The scent of the flowers is sublime, enhanced by the fact they bloom in winter when there's not much to stimulate our nostrils.

pollinated by the noctuid moth, the largest of the Lepidoptera family. In addition, red squirrels eat the seeds.

Medicinal Uses

Native Americans have traditionally used this plant for just about everything: to cure coughs and colds; as an emetic; to cure dysentery; to treat asthma, toothache and sore eyes; and to ease bruising. It was the Native Americans who brought witch hazel's medicinal values to the settlers' attention. Latter-day uses include as cream to alleviate haemorrhoids and to ease skin conditions such as eczema. Witch hazel is haemostatic, which means that it can stop the flow of blood, so it is also useful for nose bleeds. Distilled witch hazel can be applied topically to sooth bruised skin. Witch hazel is now rarely administered internally, because of the vomiting caused by the high tannin content. Pharmacies still sell witch hazel over the counter for the relief of cuts, bruises, strains, minor scalding and insect stings and bites; as well as easing pain, it also reduces swelling. A dilution of witch hazel can be used as an eyewash.

Hamamelis virginiana

WITCH HAZEL TINCTURE

Witch hazel is marvellous as a skin conditioner. Here's a simple recipe that will make your skin feel fresh and bright.

Soak a small handful of witch hazel bark in 500ml (17fl oz/2 cups) distilled water for 30 minutes. Then, pour the water and the bark into a non-reactive pan. Bring to the boil, quickly turn down the heat, put the lid on the pan and simmer for another 10 minutes or so. Allow to cool, then strain, bottle and refrigerate. Dilute 50/50 with distilled water. Use with cotton buds.

WITCH HAZEL AND COMFREY CREAM

This recipe is from my friend Rowan McOnegal, who is a brilliant herbalist and knows about pretty much everything! She tells me that the cream can be used externally for varicose veins and haemorroids as well as a face cream, so you might want to make two separate pots and mark them clearly...

You will need:

50ml (1¾fl oz/3½ tbsp) infused comfrey oil (this is simply a large handful of comfrey, either fresh or dried, put into a jar, topped up with organic sunflower oil and left for a week or so)

20g (⅔oz) cocoa butter
6g (⅛oz) beeswax
45ml (1½fl oz/3 tbsp) Witch Hazel Tincture (see page 185), from bark or young twigs
20ml (⅔fl oz) aloe vera gel
2 drops lavender essential oil

1. Melt the comfrey oil, cocoa butter and beeswax together in a bowl over a bain marie and remove from the heat when melted. Set aside.
2. Mix the witch hazel decoction and aloe vera gel in another bowl.
3. Both mixtures need to be at approximately blood temperature – the oils just beginning to harden or go opaque around the edge of the pan. Then, drizzle the oils together, mixing with a hand-held blender. Stop when it reaches the consistency of thick cream.
4. Add the drops of essential oil and stir.
5. Put into clean jars and label. Store in the fridge until needed.

Yew

Taxus baccata

Song: "A Day in the Life of a Tree" by The Beach Boys

It is very important that you don't confuse the yew with any other tree, because this tree, wrapped as it is in mysterious tales and legends of magic and sorcery, must strictly NOT be eaten. It's the only tree in this book that carries such a caveat. Apart from one tiny part (see below) this tree is highly toxic to people and most animals, with a few notable exceptions (see Wildlife, below).

Just because a tree (or, indeed, any plant) is poisonous, it's not something we should be afraid of. A yew tree isn't going to wrestle its roots out of the ground and hurl itself across a graveyard to attack you, is it? We can still admire the tree for many reasons, such as its beauty, its longevity, and as a habitat for insects, birds and mammals. Wood turners and furniture makers respect the tree for its beautiful rose-red timber, and generally wear a face mask when working with it to avoid inhaling the fine particles.

A few years ago, Theo, a good friend of mine, had an embarrassing moment while browsing in an antique shop with a (recently-acquired) girlfriend. He came across a gorgeous yew cabinet, which was coloured a rich golden orangey-red. Admiring the silky sheen, he said. "I love yew". His girlfriend went all dewy-eyed and replied "Oh Theo! I love YOU, too!" Dumbstruck, Theo then compounded the matter by hastily telling his girlfriend that he'd been admiring the cabinet, not her. Unsurprisingly, the relationship juddered to a halt at that point, which was awkward as they'd booked a B&B for another night. I don't know whether he bought the cabinet or not, though.

One of the best-known uses of yew wood is for making long bows. In fact, the use of the tree for making this simple weapon is something that human beings discovered quite some time ago. Simple self-bows (bows using a single piece of wood), dating back to Neolithic times and made from lots of different kinds of timber, have been found in many parts of the world. The most ancient example found thus far was discovered next to a naturally mummified corpse, nicknamed Otzi, found in the Tyrolean Alps and dated to some 3,300 years BC.

A long bow is precisely that – as tall as the archer who shoots the arrows, each one a bespoke weapon made to suit the bearer. For it to be a truly elite weapon, the wood that a longbow is made from needs to be both very strong and very flexible, so that the arrow can be pulled back to effect maximum trajectory toward the enemy. Someone, somewhere, once used yew for this purpose and discovered that he or she had made the most effective bow yet. Historically, we know, too, that Native Americans, as well as

Europeans, used yew to make the best longbows. This is a case of people in different parts of the planet experimenting and coming to the same conclusion – yet another reminder that we are all pretty much the same!

For those who like their facts and figures about their trees to be totally accurate, the yew is something of a conundrum. The heartwood of the tree rots away from the inside, taking with it the ability for us to carbon date it; furthermore, the yew can't be measured by its rings because of the way the tree grows. This means that claims of epic longevity for ancient yew trees may not be accurate. Despite that, we can still make a rough estimate of a yew's age by looking at its surroundings and by taking comparable samples of timber used in ancient buildings. Also, most importantly, we can gauge it by the tales told about a particular tree.

What does it look like?

The yew grows to a height of 20m (66ft), with a spread of 10m (33ft). It's an evergreen, with dark green needles 3cm (1¼in) long, that look almost black from a distance. The bark is a purple or brown colour, with a habit of flaking. The yew often has several trunks, and the overall shape is triangular. Clusters of the tiny pale yellow male flowers appear in the spring beneath the shoots, while the equally small, pale green female flowers are carried singly at the ends of the shoots, on separate plants. The fruit, which ripens in the autumn months, is a single black seed surrounded by a bright red, fleshy covering called an "aril". The yew grows in an interesting way, leaving a hollow inside the tree as the bark expands outward. It's often easy to climb into a hollow yew; when it rains, the smooth internal bark turns a deep scarlet, like blood.

And here I'd like to introduce you, in words, to one of the yew trees I walk past most mornings while exercising my dog (and myself). This tree is in an avenue of nine similar trees that were planted at roughly the same time as the church was built, just over a thousand years ago. In Europe, most churchyards have a yew somewhere nearby. There are lots of suppositions about why the trees are there, which I'll come to shortly. "My"' yew, to the right of the path that leads to the door of the church, is a real stunner. It isn't massively tall, but has a deep hollow inside which, to the sharp-eyed, contains a litter of delightful finds: bird feathers, a decoration from a Christmas tree from long ago and a tiny silver brooch etched with an ivy leaf that I recently found and buried inside – something for someone from the future to find and wonder about. When it rains, the smooth twist of timber inside the hollow glows a deep blood red from the water that pours into it. This tree is at odds with itself, at once gnarly and smooth, and twisty and straight; it's covered with scruffy little "beards" of its needle-like leaves; and the ends of the branches develop into tiny "wooden" flowers, a bouquet for an elf. This tree looks like wind and water solidified. No human being could ever sculpt something so randomly beautiful.

And so I started thinking about our yew trees. They were – and are – considered to be caught somewhere between the realms of life and death, part of both worlds, somehow. I see signs, whether we admit it or not, that people love trees (after all, you're reading this book) and it isn't too much of a massive step to suppose that we also worship them, even though we might not call it that. My theory is that such a noticeable and long-lived tree would have been part of the landscape down through the ages, for simpler folk with more common sense than us, who didn't travel as far and wide as we do now. For them, the tree would have been a place of worship, as well as a meeting place and, of course, a sort of vertical playground for the kids who immediately appreciated its potential for climbing.

So, what has changed about this tree? Nothing – in the same way that nothing has changed about us. The earliest churches would have been built where the yew tree grew – where the footfall for worship existed already, where people already considered the place to be sacred because the tree was regarded as a part of their family.

There's more. Although I started by warning you of the dangerous toxicity of this tree, there's something else. One of the most effective cancer treatments, a drug called Taxol, is found in the bark of the Pacific yew tree, and a similar compound was discovered in the European yew. The drugs were once made from needle clippings, but we've now learned to synthesize the active chemicals in a laboratory instead. And so the yew tree, known as the tree of life and death, will kill but it will also cure. It's as though its mythical past was right all the time.

But – please – avoid touching it and DON'T eat it!

Wildlife

Humans, horses, cattle, cats, dogs and many other mammals die if they ingest yew. However, squirrels and dormice feast on the berries, as do birds such as mistle thrushes, fieldfares, blackbirds and song thrushes, which also nest amid the dense, protective branches. Yew leaves are eaten by satin beauty moth caterpillars.

Medicinal Uses

Owing to its toxicity, the yew does not have a tradition as a natural medicine. However, modern science discovered a compound in yew needles that has helped in the fight against cancer (see above).

LEARNING ABOUT TOXIC PLANTS

Those of you with beady eyes will notice that I told you all parts of the yew tree – except for one – are toxic. Some of you may be wondering what that one part might be. It's the "aril", the pinky-red,

Taxus baccata

fleshy berry that surrounds the small, black, highly toxic stone. However, I would still advise caution here, as there are several accounts of people vomiting after eating the aril. Birds love them, though, so I'd recommend you leave them to our feathered friends.

As foragers, we tend to concentrate on edible plants. However, it's also very useful to arm yourself with information about plants that are toxic. You could start to compile an ongoing list of plants that are poisonous and not to be eaten (or even touched), but that, like the yew, have a powerful medicinal use. If you want to use tree and plant identification apps, there are plenty out there, but please make sure that you have at least three different sources, and one of them is a reputable book, such as *Wicked Plants* by Amy Stewart. Comparing a book, an app and another source such as the internet will stand you in good stead for your foraging adventures.

1,000-YEAR TIMELINE CONTEMPLATION

This is not so much an activity as a contemplation, designed to get you thinking about yew trees, time and what it is to be human. Do we ever really change? I don't think so. The selections here are fairly random, starting a thousand years ago and ending in 2021. And while all these profound or crazy things were happening, the yew tree in the churchyard, which I see most days, was already old.

Whenever I get anxious or worried, I think of this. It's a reminder to simply be in the moment, because that's really all we ever have.

1066 – The Norman Conquest of Britain
1215 – The Magna Carta is signed
1300s – Italian Renaissance begins
1347–51 – Peak spread of bubonic plague in Europe
1438 – Incan Empire formed in Peru
1455 – Gutenberg Press prints The Bible
1492 – Columbus reaches the New World
1519 – Aztec Empire at its height as Spanish arrive
1603 – *Hamlet* by William Shakespeare is published
1648 – The Taj Mahal is completed
1721 – J S Bach completes the Brandenberg Concertos
1776 – US Declaration of Independence adopted
1795 – Edward Jenner creates smallpox vaccine
1826 – Joseph Niépce takes the first photograph
1833 – Slavery abolished in the British Empire
1867 – Japan's Shogun Empire ends
1885 – World's first skyscraper built in Chicago
1903 – Wright Brothers fly the first motorized airplane
1914 – World War I begins
1929 – US stock market crashes, triggering a global depression
1945 – Atom bombs drop on Hiroshima and Nagasaki
1949 – Communist victory in China
1957 – Soviet Union launches Sputnik 1, the first artificial satellite
1969 – Neil Armstrong and Buzz Aldrin walk on the moon
1989 – Fall of communism in Eastern Europe
2004 – Tsunami devastates 11 Asian countries
2010 – Apple launches iPad
2012 – US Space rover Curiosity takes selfie on Mars
2019 – Covid-19 pandemic begins in Wuhan, China
2021 – This book is published

Dead Tree

Song: "Everyone Sleeps" by Hauschka

When is a tree – or anything at all, for that matter – dead? Is there any such thing as a "dead" tree? Unlike a mammal, whose expiration is fairly conclusive, the death of a tree is much harder to determine.

It was a tree that inspired me to look into this idea – a tree that is still standing, as I'm writing this, right outside my bedroom window – a truly colossal horse chestnut. When I moved here five years ago, this particular tree was thriving, showing off in the summer with its leafy hands fluttering in the breeze like a gossipy pantomime dame, and filling my garden just a few feet away with the sublime scent of its show-off pink and white flowers in the summer. The same leaves, now turned brown, clog my gutters in the autumn as they clatter down in the wind. In my imagination I see this tree as a protective influence, standing as it does like a sentinel right opposite my garden gate. And that's to say nothing of the lifetime's supply of conkers that this tree knocks out every year. Or, rather, used to knock out.

The change was gradual. I didn't notice at first that the tree stopped growing leaves. When I did notice, my first thought was that this was just a temporary thing and the tree would be fine next year. How easy it is to delude ourselves with wishful thinking. There's no one moment that a tree dies. My friend and neighbour Sam, who works with trees and is very knowledgeable, told me that "my" tree wasn't going to recover, that sadly there are new diseases now destroying trees.

The specific issue for the horse chestnut is a little creature called the horse chestnut leaf miner, first noticed in Macedonia in the 1980s. This leaf miner isn't evil. He's just doing his job and is one part of a two-pronged attack on the horse chestnut. As well as having to cope with the leaf miner, the tree already suffers from a bacterial disease called "bleeding canker", which clogs up the veins of the leaves so that the tree, quite literally, can't breathe. In addition, the leaf miner seems to be exacerbating the effects of the canker by weakening the trees' ability to photosynthesize. As Sam was telling me all this, my eyes swivelled in the direction of another fine horse chestnut just a few metres away, which looked absolutely fine ... but for how long?

What we can salvage from this, though, is that a tree is never really "dead" in the way we might understand the concept. However, signs that a tree is transitioning are numerous: lack of leaves for a few seasons; peeling bark (the horse chestnut now has large bare patches where its bark has simply fallen away); cracks; splits; falling rotten limbs; and dead branches entangled in the tree. These are all signs. One day I climbed over two locked gates to get a closer look at the other side of the tree, to see what else might be going on. I was shocked to see a huge gash extending to a quarter of the height of the tree from which its dessicated, crumbling innards spilled out. It was a bit like an arboreal crime scene.

Despite this, the "dead"' tree acts as a series of rent-free penthouse apartments for the crows that live there; there's a family of woodpeckers, too (the baby one appears in my garden sometimes – a total imbecile who needs to be reminded most days by his dad as to how a bird feeder works); and countless squirrels flinging themselves around like little furry acrobats. So, there's a lot of life in those brittle, leafless branches. And what I can see is just the tip of the iceberg.

A dead tree is "dead wood", and it can stay standing for some time – I'm sure you've seen trees like this. A dead or dying tree is also called a "snag". Sometimes, people deliberately leave part of the trunk of a dead tree at a decent (but safe) height, specifically so that birds can perch on it. However, sometimes a dead tree will simply fall; I've seen this just once, when a Japanese larch standing right at the edge of the forest, which was part of an abandoned forestry plantation, slowly started to fall, groaning, gaining speed rapidly as it knocked down two other trees in its wake. It made huge banging and crashing sounds, setting off a flurry of alarmed birds. With the larch, it was interesting to see just how shallow the soil that these tall trees had been growing in was. In a very dry summer, the soil can shrink away from the roots of a living tree – a bit like a wobbly tooth in your gum – leaving the tree unstable.

A dead tree can fall for a number of reasons: a heavy wind or a storm can blow it down, as can a dramatic fall of snow. As soon as the tree hits the ground, whatever the reason, contact with the soil makes it damp, accelerating the rot; then the tree becomes host to all sorts of insects and beetles, providing food for the birds. As dead wood decomposes, it helps new plants to grow by returning essential nutrients into the eco-system. The fallen, rotting leaves also provide conditions in which fungi can grow. And most of all, underneath the ground, even a dead tree is still part of the mycorrhizal network, also known as the wood-wide web (which is also a heck of a lot easier to spell). This network makes the internet look positively clunky. It is composed of tiny filaments of fungi all working together to provide nutrients where they are needed, sometimes borrowing from one tree to support another that might need a particular nutrient more urgently. These tiny organisms are "mutualisms", formed between the fungi and the plant. To give you an idea of the scope of this invisible network, if you are standing on the ground on one foot, there will be 300 miles of mycorrhizae beneath that foot. It's also very important that forests and woods – and indeed, gardens – aren't too tidy. We need both life and death to sustain not only the garden, but the entire garden that is this planet.

So, am I still sad that "my" horse chestnut is going to be cut down one day soon? Yes, I am. But it's not the end of the world. It's the cycle of life, which is neither cruel, nor kind, but what we make it.

The beautiful illustration, here, is of the actual tree that inspired this chapter. As I sit here, right now, on a blustery autumn day, I can still see the tree. By the time you read this, the skyline for me will have changed. But I'll still have the picture.

BUG HOTEL

If you spot pieces of a dead or decaying tree while on a walk, make a note of the location and go back with a bag. Collect slivers of bark, chunks of crumbling or rotting wood and sticks to make a bug hotel.

Your structure doesn't need to be confined to a boxy shape like a commercially bought bug hotel. Simply find an accessible, sheltered spot and pile up everything you've collected, breaking up the wood with bits of sticks or reeds to aerate the stack. Go back to visit occasionally and add extra "rooms" to your bug hotel.

CONCLUSION:
How to Make Friends with a Tree
Song: "Hunger of the Pine" by alt-J

By now, I hope that you have fallen a little more in love with trees than you already were (I'm assuming that if you have bought this book, you must be interested in them already). If so, you might want to take things a step further.

I'm not suggesting that you go as far as the Mexican women (and one man) who, in a mass wedding ceremony in 2018, dressed all in white and "married" their favourite trees, even throwing bouquets, just like real brides. This was part of a publicity stunt to draw attention to logging practices which, despite being illegal, were still being carried out in the state of Oaxaca. By "marrying" the trees the brides hoped to draw attention to the rapidly diminishing forests.

I'm not suggesting that you take to hugging trees, either (although it is rather nice), but you might be interested to know how the term came about. In 1730, 294 men and 69 women of the Vishnoi branch of the Hindu faith came together to stop their trees being used to build a palace. They physically clung to the trees to prevent them being cut down.

All I'm asking is that you choose a tree you pass by every day – the sort of tree that's such a familiar a part of the landscape you don't even notice, but that you would miss if it suddenly disappeared. It could be a lone tree by the side of the road, or you might be lucky enough to have a tree in your garden. It could be young or old, tall or short, deciduous or evergreen. It might even be one of the "dead" trees discussed elsewhere in this book, which people are often fond of (see page 194).

Once you start to look more closely you will discover features that you have never seen before. I've noticed that sometimes the way the light from the sun shines on a tree means that hitherto-unnoticed details come to light, such as a fissure in the bark of an oak that's deeper than you thought, or maybe the dazzling green colour of a freshly unfurled beech leaf.

If you like, you can record what you see each day in a notebook. You don't need to write volumes – just a line or maybe even a sketch, will do. The idea is to observe the subtle changes that happen every day – tiny things. Don't worry if you miss a few days. This isn't a competition. A further way to pay attention to your particular tree is to take a picture every day, too. If you are able to, take a photo from the same spot every day and, after a year, you'll end up with a dramatically beautiful series of images (maybe you could compile these into a film).

Strangely, this kind of close observation makes you look at other aspects of life, too. The changes you see in the tree run alongside the river of your own life. It's a thoughtful practice that is equally as good for children as for adults.

Let me give you a brief example of my own tree observation from this morning. I'm lucky enough to live in the countryside where there are lots of trees, and a couple of hours ago I took my little border collie Lis for our favourite walk in a field bounded by trees along the edge of a river. It's late October, and there's a slight drizzle. Lis' fur is glistening with tiny beads of misty rain. I left the house at 6:45am and now it's about 7 o'clock, still not particularly light.

There's something about the misty rain and the early morning light that's making one tree stand out from the rest. It's a tall, slim beech, without much of a canopy as it is crowded by other trees. This crowding means that the trunk of the tree, maybe just a metre or so in diameter, is absolutely tall and straight, unlike the surrounding trees. The smooth grey bark is untarnished, pale, secure. The feeling I get from this tree is one of clarity, strength and security.

Although I am aware that we humans like to superimpose all sorts of feelings and notions onto the natural world, this isn't such a bad thing. The feeling of calm inspired by this encounter is very encouraging and helps me to map out all the things I need to do today, giving me clarity. One of those was to write this. I've had so many ideas for this book that I wasn't sure what to do next. Taking that walk and meeting the tree sorted out everything that had been spinning around in my mind like a jigsaw puzzle without the finished image on the lid to provide guidance. Now I know what the picture is.

Shinrin Yoku or Forest Bathing

You might have heard about this practice, which originated in Japan and is also called forest bathing. The Japanese term *shinrin yoku* – which translates as "forest bath" – goes back to the middle Chinese period (5th–12th centuries AD), when it was called *senlinyu*, so this practice has its roots not only in Japan but also in China and Korea.

We all know that being in nature makes us feel better, but when such an activity has a name, its importance is underscored. You might want to read more about Dr Qing Li and his findings about "inhaling the forest atmosphere", which leads to measurable beneficial changes in the human body (see *The Biophilia Effect,* listed in Further Reading, page 204). In short, pine trees give off naturally occurring substances called terpenes, which have a fresh, soothing, clear scent and are anti-fungal, anti-bacterial and anti-inflammatory. By putting ourselves into the middle of a pine forest and simply breathing in the atmosphere, we give our immune system a boost and our sense of wellbeing is enhanced, too. Qing Li's findings were that the effects of just one hour in the forest, once every two weeks, were enough to keep us "bolstered".

There are forest bathing practitioners springing up all over the world, and having a guide is great, but here is an idea of what you need to do if you either can't find one or would prefer to do it for yourself.

Forest bathing is a slow, conscious practice. It is very simple. If you want to try it, leave all phones and devices behind and allow yourself to be as free as you possibly can. We don't always pay attention to our senses, because we can live very much "in our heads". By focusing on each of our senses, one at a time, we can achieve a profound sense of waking relaxation. The beauty of this sort of nature therapy is that even if any of your senses are impaired, as long as you can breathe, you will benefit.

First, be clear in your mind that in this practice you are opening yourself to the natural world as one of the many creatures that belongs to it. To mark the transition between your everyday life and this more truthful way of being, choose a natural boundary. This could be as simple as a stick lying on the ground, a gate, a stone or anything similar. Breathe slowly, deeply and consciously throughout.

- **Sight:** Look around you, slowly gazing at your surroundings as though you've never seen them before. Notice the colours you can see and find new names for them if you wish. Appreciate how the light strikes certain features of the landscape or how the mist makes everything look mysterious, or whatever inspires you. Gaze at the colours of the tree you've chosen, the fissures in the bark, the edges of the leaves … and so on.
- **Sound:** If you can, sit on the ground with your back against the tree, and pay attention to the sounds you can hear. Are there birds singing? Water running? A booming river, a dripping puddle, wind rustling in trees and branches? You may hear the sounds of traffic, too – acknowledge them and let them go.
- **Touch:** Here's where you get to know your tree by touching it with your eyes closed. Stroke the bark, feeling your way into interstices or fissures. Run your hands over mosses and lichens. The bark – is it rough or smooth, wet or dry, somewhere in between? Take your time to feel the tree.
- **Smell:** Again, sit down if you can, close your eyes and lean against the tree. The sense of smell is very important, often relaying messages from the outside world to our subconscious

mind. Bring this sense to the surface and let your imagination take over. Breathe slowly and deeply. What odours do you detect? What do you think they are? Sniff leaves, grasses, mosses and pinches of soil … you may find that these scents make you recall your childhood.

- **Taste:** This works well if you have even a basic knowledge of edible wild plants. Tasting things that grow wild is always fun, but make sure you are trying only NON–TOXIC plants. (If in any doubt, don't taste it!) Eating something wild during a forest bathing session can really link you to where you are.

You can also bring something with you as a treat or for lunch; you might want to scatter some crumbs for birds or other animals.

Forest bathing sessions tend to get slower as you relax, and that's the whole point. You don't need to go very far at all; this is not a test of endurance or a race of any kind! As you walk back to your starting point, you'll find that the magic of taking real notice of the natural world stays with you, and you bring it back to illuminate your home and workplace with its peace and accessibility.

Don't worry about identifying the trees. It's not always easy. They may have been pruned, or bits might have fallen off. They might be covered in ivy, or they could have grown into an unusual shape as a result of the circumstances they have lived through.

And the best thing about forest bathing is that even if you can't find a pine forest, being among any trees at all will soothe your mind and stimulate your senses, enhancing your sense of wellbeing. Try it for yourself and you'll see what I mean.

Before I Go...

I wanted to briefly mention some of the trees that were not included in this book. The Japanese Larch, for instance. Unusually, it's a deciduous conifer tree that loses its needles in the winter, unlike "normal" conifers. As the winter turns to spring, its tiny little flowers (which eventually grow into equally tiny cones) turn from green to yellow to red, giving the tree a rainbow-like haze if you catch it at the right moment.

Or how about the alder, which loves to have its feet in water, and is highly resistant to rotting? Much of Venice was built on alder piles. Also, alder's long catkins are the most glorious shade of purple in late winter, quite dazzling.

I've been lucky enough to see sequoia trees (giant redwoods) in the US Pacific coastal area. The fact that they are protected is down to John Muir, a naturalist and writer, who understood their value. In May 1903, he persuaded President Theodore Roosevelt to take a three-day hike into the Yosemite wilderness, to see the trees for himself. The first night saw them bed down underneath the canopy of a particularly impressive tree, The Grizzly Giant, some 63.7m (209ft) high.

During the trip there was significant snowfall; at night, bundled up in blankets, far away from all the trappings of office, Roosevelt sat by a crackling fine as Muir persuaded the President that the area needed protection. To cut a long story short, Mariposa Grove and the Yosemite Valley were officially made part of the Yosemite National Park. And, in case you're wondering, the Grizzly Giant is still there, still protected.

These are but a few of the other wonderful trees out there and I know that there are many, many more tree stories to be told. I hope you've enjoyed reading mine and that you find your own stories in the trees you love to forage and live with, too.

"The Buddha achieved enlightenment while meditating under a tree. To what extent did the tree's being contribute to the Buddha's shift of consciousness?"
Melina Sempill Watts, from her book Tree

Further Reading

Arvay, Clemens G *The Biophilia Effect,* Sounds True, Louisville (CO), USA, 2018

Bartram, Thomas *Bartram's Encyclopedia of Herbal Medicine,* Robinson, London, 1998

Brooks, Craig *Eat Like a Viking!* Amazon, UK, 2020

Cisar-Erlach, Artur *The Flavor of Wood,* Abrams Press, New York, 2019

Deakin, Roger *Wildwood – A Journey Through Trees,* Penguin, London, 2007

Giono, Jean *The Man Who Planted Trees,* Harvill Press, London, new edition 1995

Gooley, Tristan *The Walker's Guide to Outdoor Clues and Signs,* Sceptre, London, 2015

Hart-Davies, Christina *The Greenwood Trees,* Two Rivers Press, Reading, UK, 2018

Haskell, David George *The Songs of Trees,* Penguin, London, 2017

Hurst, Kim *Hidden Histories – Herbs,* Timber Press, Portland (OR), USA, 2015

Logan, Jason *Make Ink – A Forager's Guide to Natural Ink Making,* Abrams Press, New York, 2018

Mabey, Richard *Flora Brittanica,* Sinclair-Stevenson, London, 1996

Miles, Archie *Silva,* Ebury Press, London, 1999

Packenham, Thomas *Remarkable Trees of the World,* Weidenfeld & Nicholson, London, 2002

Penn, Robert *The Many Who Made Things Out of Trees,* Penguin, London, 2015

Preston, Richard *The Wild Trees,* Allen Lane, London, 2007

Rackham, Oliver *Woodlands,* William Collins, London, 2006

Stewart, Amy *Wicked Plants,* Timber Press, Portland (OR), USA, 2010

Wohlieben, Peter *The Hidden Life of Trees,* William Collins, London, 2017

Resources (see also Acknowledgements, opposite)

The Woodland Trust (woodlandtrust.org.uk)

My friends at Plantlife (plantlife.org.uk)

Plants for a Future (pfaf.org)

Contact the Author

You can contact me at:
Breconbeaconsforaging@gmail.com and www.BreconbeaconsForaging.com

Contact the Illustrator

You can contact Lizzie Harper at:
info@lizzieharper.co.uk and www.lizzieharper.co.uk

Acknowledgements

My heartfelt thanks go to the following people:

Fiona Robertson, for intuition, listening and always being there even during excitable early morning messages. Thanks also to everyone at Watkins, including Brittany Willis and Rebecca Woods, and an especially deep bow to Ingrid Court-Jones who managed to transform the task of making sense of the manuscript into something that was fun and enjoyable – for me, at least. Oh, and especially for the idea about planting monkey puzzle trees!

Rowan McOnegal, medical herbalist, who advised about certain aspects of tincture and ointment-making. I would highly recommend her courses in plant medicine, perfumery and more. Contact her via Instagram (hedgerowpharmacy) or hedgerowmedicine.org.

Sir Andrew and Lady Susan Large, who showed me their beautiful apple orchards and generously gave me medlars and quinces to experiment with. In doing so they inadvertently taught me a great deal. That lovely autumn day was one of the inspirations for this book.

All my friends at the Talybont on Usk Woodland Groups, especially Gareth Ellis and Charles Weston.

Sam and Lucy, for Sam's information, but mainly because they named their little girl Tilia.

The Watercress Queen, for letting me use her conker wash liquid recipe.

Gavin, Vina, Forrest, Josh and Olive at The Penpont Project www.actionforconservation.org

Robert Penn, Jill and all at Stump Up for Trees www.stumpupfortrees.org.

Andy Dix at www.twmpacycles.co.uk.

Gavin and Prue Kellett at Ty'r Gobaith Preserves.

Rachel Cadman, for happy days playing with dyes and inks.

Harry Chapman, woodturner to princes, for general advice about woody stuff.

Kim Walker and her colleagues at Kew – Clare Drinkell, Christina Hourighan and George Smale, – who made great efforts to help me find out certain information I needed to know www.kew.org.

All my colleagues at The Association of Foragers, and especially those who provided recipes for the Sea Buckthorn chapter – Lisa Cutliffe at www.eduliswildfood.co.uk, Andy Knott of Wild Food Dorset. I'd also like to thank Andy Hamilton www.theotherandyhamilton.com.

Racheal Phillips for keeping my website spick and span, and Colm Fitzpatrick at Fitzaudio.com for filming aspects of this book.

All those who showed me different ways of making Viking whisks, especially Craig (whose book Eat Like a Viking is a must-read) and Max Levy. Christmas will never be the same!

Rosalind and Jeff Garratt, who gave me lots of walnuts to play with.

Tim Husom at Red Bird Music.

Volker for writing a thought-provoking and wonderful insight into his thought processes.

Lizzie Harper, not only for illustrating this book exquisitely, but for going the extra mile, again and again and again, always with good humour and a sprinkle of glitter.

Liam, for feeding me and letting me use some of his recipes, and to my dog Lis, who is always happy to come on a yomp to look at some trees.

Yolanta, Michaelis and all the LowBap crew.

Also, for Clark Datchler's beautiful words and music.

"When I am searching for inspiration, when I am in doubt, when I am elated and when I am in pain, I go to the trees. I sit with them and they don't judge me for my chaotic human experience. In fact, I think they understand me, as a grandparent does a grandchild."
Clark Datchler, 2021

INDEX